THE PRIORITY
OF RETIREMENT

THE PRIORITY OF RETIREMENT
How to Align Your Financial Future Using the Wisdom of the Ages

ISBN (paperback): 978-1-964046-09-9
ISBN (hardcover): 978-1-964046-06-8

Expert
Press
www.ExpertPress.net

Editing by Jarmila Gorman
Copyediting by Wendy Lukasiewicz
Proofreading by Geena Barret
Text design and composition by Emily Fritz
Cover design by Casey Fritz

THE PRIORITY OF RETIREMENT

How to Align Your Financial Future
Using the Wisdom of the Ages

SHAWN MALONEY

I thank my Savior Jesus Christ for His love and grace and the blessing to do what I love.

No words can describe the appreciation I have for my wife, Debbie, who supported and encouraged me to pursue my joy and my passion. I love you!

Many are the plans in the mind of a man, but it is the purpose of the Lord that will stand (Proverbs 19:21 ESV).

CONTENTS

Retirement is becoming a period of life that is a combination of relaxing and striving for more activity and purpose, as many seem to be realizing.

———

INTRODUCTION

———

Did you know that the notion of retirement is still in its infancy?

According to a 2025 article in *Time Magazine*, the idea of retirement didn't become popular until the passage of Social Security in 1935.[1] That might sound like a long time ago, but it means only a handful of generations have even tested the retirement waters. So let yourself off the hook if you're feeling uneasy about the future, and congratulations on being on the cutting edge.

It's easy to understand why retirement gained popularity so rapidly. The typical American worked about seventy hours a week in the 1850s. A significant portion of that labor was truly backbreaking. From this perspective, the relaxation that retirement offered was a boon.

———

[1] James Chappel, "History's Lesson for Making Retirement More Meaningful," *Time*, January 3, 2025, https://time.com/7198601/retirement-history.

Even though retirement is still a relatively new idea, our lifestyles are significantly different from our grandparents'. The times have dramatically changed. Retirement is becoming a period of life that is a combination of relaxing and striving for more activity and purpose, as many seem to be realizing.

Prioritizing retirement planning is more crucial than ever, regardless of your interests (traveling the world, taking up new hobbies, hanging out with loved ones, volunteering, etc.). Prioritizing planning is especially vital if you're not sure you have enough money saved up to get you through potentially two to three decades without a paycheck.

Most people put the cart before the horse—they plan out their finances for retirement first and focus on core pursuits, relationships, and health later. If you want a fulfilling retirement, all areas should be developed in tandem. You have to know what you want and how you're going to fund it.

Unfortunately, retirement planning is a complex proposition. Today's retirement plans are a far cry from our parents' or grandparents' retirement plans, which typically centered on a pension plan. That has all but gone away, with fewer than 20 percent of companies offering pensions, and many people not being eligible because of the current culture of changing jobs every few years.[2] Today's risks are different; the plan has to be different too.

---

2   An Expert Explains Why Companies Have Moved Away from Pensions and Toward 401ks," Investopedia, April 6, 2025, https://www.investopedia.com/what-s-the-difference-between-pension-and-401k-and-why-are-companies-moving-away-from-pensions-11707094.

According to a Yahoo! Finance article in 2019, 64 percent of Americans will retire broke. Another 19 percent will retire with less than $10,000. This means that in 2019 only 17 percent of Americans had the luxury of living a comfortable retirement that meets not only their financial needs but also their emotional needs.[3]

As a result many Americans are delaying retirement, and some are unable to retire at all. Many of those who do retire live at or below the poverty level. A recent survey by Pew Research found that one-fifth of retirement-aged Americans continue to hold a job, nearly twice as many as those who were working in 1987.[4] Some choose to remain employed to stay productive. Others don't have a choice.

You may belong to this vast majority who are now looking at their golden years with fear of running out of money. Or maybe you're younger, and you still have time to build up a retirement nest egg. Or you managed to save and invest enough for retirement, but you don't have a clear plan on how to spend your money.

Either way, whatever your situation, I want to emphasize one thing: Start planning now, no matter your age.

What can you do if you've reached retirement age, and you have nothing much to show for it? This book will

---

3   Sean Dennison, "64% of Americans Aren't Prepared For Retirement — and 48% Don't Care," September 23, 2019, Yahoo! Finance, https://finance.yahoo.com/news/survey-finds-42-americans-retire-100701878.html.

4   Richard Fry and Dana Braga, "Older Workers Are Growing in Number and Earning Higher Wages," December 14, 2023, Pew Research Center, https://www.pewresearch.org/social-trends/2023/12/14/older-workers-are-growing-in-number-and-earning-higher-wages/,

illustrate that even if you have no savings, you can improve your situation. If you're in good shape financially, this book can help you make the best use of your money so that you're adequately funded for your retirement.

Retirement planning isn't something most people can do themselves. As I've mentioned, today's retirement planning is complex. One of the main reasons that retirement planning is essential is that most people don't account for everything. I've seen this countless times. A client comes to me giddy with excitement, planning their first few years of retirement (the Go-Go Years), but they've neglected how they'll properly disburse and draw down their retirement funds, and they've neglected the health care costs of getting old. And those costs add up.

Working with a trusted retirement planner can help set you up for a great retirement. Even if you haven't planned up until now, or weren't able to save enough money, we can still do things together that can improve the outlook.

I wrote this book as a guide to help you understand ways to apply time-tested and proven principles to your financial situation, whatever it may be, and to give you a better grasp of the priority of retirement.

But having enough money for retirement is only part of the equation. This book will discuss the fundamentals of retirement planning:

- Setting specific retirement goals
- Budgeting for retirement goals

- Understanding and following the principles of the Treasure Target
- Establishing proper priorities to avoid unpleasant surprises or financial devastation
- Using debt properly
- Achieving the retirement happy factor
- Understanding generous giving and why it's a key component of happiness

All this and much more, to give you the knowledge to confidently fund your retirement.

How Can I Help?

We all work hard for our lifestyle, and we give so much to our careers. Everyone deserves a happy retirement. What does your retirement happiness look like? What is your vision and purpose in retirement? No matter how much money you have or how little, everyone needs a personalized, comprehensive retirement plan that factors in how they would like to live out their golden years.

The younger you start, the better, but it doesn't matter if you're twenty-five or sixty-five. The need for a proper plan is still there. I would be honored to work with you in creating your retirement plan.

I'm passionate about helping people get ready for retirement. Readiness includes doing a proper analysis and defining a plan that accounts for the growth/accumulation phase and the distribution/drawdown phase. I also consider the non-financial aspects of retirement planning.

With extensive experience in the financial services industry, I began my career in banking, financial technology and compliance, evolving over time to focus on insurance, financial and retirement planning, and then founded Retire Wise, LLC. I base my counsel on principles that have proven effective over time, even in this more volatile modern age when most people don't have a steady pension to count on. It's a time-honored approach, yet one that is in keeping with the current situation.

I've been enthusiastic about retirement and financial planning for a long time. While I was working in a corporate job, I heard God's call to drop what I was doing and go full time with my own company. My insights and viewpoints have been featured in prominent publications such as Yahoo! Finance, USA Today, and Kiplinger, as well as on local affiliates of major TV networks including NBC, ABC, FOX, and CBS. As a financial planner, I strive to help my clients pursue their financial goals and achieve a comfortable retirement lifestyle.

A big part of my service is education. I don't just present a bunch of numbers and strategies to my clients; I educate them in the practical aspects of a particular strategy, and I explain how it supports their "why," or the dream they have for their retirement years. What I teach is easy to comprehend and, more importantly, easy to apply. By the time you finish reading this book, you may feel confident enough to manage your own retirement plan, or you may feel that working with a trusted financial advisor will help you optimize what you have so you can get where you want to be.

Case Study: Marcus and Cindy

At Retire Wise, LLC, we believe in a comprehensive approach to retirement planning that helps our clients to grow and preserve their retirement savings. You've worked hard your whole life and deserve a great retirement. Our Retire Happy Framework™ has been instrumental in guiding our clients toward a stable financial future. The framework focuses not only on the financial aspects but also the non-financial aspects of retirement to help our clients retire happy, fulfilled, and secure. This case study focuses on one of our client couples, Marcus and Cindy, who successfully used our framework to achieve their retirement goals.

Marcus, a fifty-year-old marketing professional, and Cindy, a forty-eight-year-old nonprofit organization builder, have both been successful in their respective careers. Despite this, they had little saved for retirement and no clear retirement plan in place. They were deeply invested in personal development and driven by their goal of achieving financial freedom. They were worried about their future and retirement years, and because of a lavish lifestyle, the couple didn't have enough of a nest egg to last throughout their retirement. Because of past experiences and setbacks, they were skeptical about financial planning services.

Marcus and Cindy needed a comprehensive approach that would address all their needs, which is exactly what our Retire Happy Framework™ is designed to provide. It focuses on growing and preserving retirement savings, while also anticipating the non-financial aspects of lifestyle planning, retirement goals and purpose, health considerations, and legacy planning.

We introduced Marcus and Cindy to the Retire Happy Framework™, and we worked closely with them to understand their financial situation, goals, and concerns. Our comprehensive approach to retirement planning includes the following actions:

- Analysis of their current financial situation
- Clarification of their retirement goals
- Development of a personalized plan to help achieve these goals

We focused on the non-financial aspects first. We helped Marcus and Cindy envision their lifestyle in retirement: where they wanted to live, how they wanted to spend their time, what their goals and dreams were, and what legacy they wanted to leave behind. We also discussed potential health issues and longevity expectations based on their family history and the importance of having a health care plan. This helped clarify what their retirement could look like.

We then turned our attention to the financial side. Armed with their retirement goals in mind, we worked with

Marcus and Cindy to develop a personalized financial plan that included investment strategies, tax planning, and risk management that fit into and coexisted with the retirement they had defined earlier.

After going through the framework coaching and working with us, Marcus and Cindy are now well on their way to achieving their retirement goals. They have a robust financial plan that gives them confidence about their financial future. They went from a 45 percent probability retirement success rate to over 90 percent, determined from running their new plan through both a historical analysis simulation and Monte Carlo simulations. They have a clearer vision of their retirement and are taking the steps to make it a reality. The comprehensive approach of The Retire Happy Framework™ helped them be more prepared and excited for their retirement.

You only have one chance to create a rewarding and fulfilling life. To enjoy this next chapter of your life—the retirement years—you must plan for it properly. Starting now.

Let's dive in.

As you move into
the next phase of life,
I encourage you to
pause and be grateful
for where you are,
even if it's not ideal.

———

SECTION 1

———

Foundation

I want to emphasize that we're planning for a retirement that can be nearly as long as your working life.

That's a long time.

Many people don't know exactly how their retirement years will pan out. They may be focused on the few "fun years" at the beginning and gloss over the latter part of retirement. Thirty years is a long time to plan for, but it's necessary to put the foundation in place.

What happens after the fun years run their course? Do you have a plan for extended health challenges? Do you have a plan in case your money runs low?

Financial planning is only one part of the retirement happiness equation.

While some people focus on what they'll be doing and don't plan how they'll pay for retirement, others plan meticulously for anticipated financial expenditures but neglect to find ways to fill their retirement years with meaning. As you move into the next phase of life, I encourage you to pause and be grateful for where you are, even if it's not ideal. We begin the process by realistically laying out what will make you happy, fulfilled, satisfied, and stress-free in retirement.

Allow yourself to dream a little.

CHAPTER 1

Your Retirement Why

Imagine it's your last couple of weeks of work. If you're like most people, you're excited and eagerly looking forward to the next chapter of your life.

Have you clarified what life will look like once you stop punching the clock? Surprisingly, many people only have a vague idea. They may imagine a few bucket-list trips, maybe spending more time with their grandkids, taking up a hobby, volunteering, or just relaxing with no alarm clock in sight.

What I've noticed is that many people don't talk about things that give their life purpose and meaning. When your survival needs are taken care of, what will your retirement money be used for? What will make you truly happy?

Knowing what you want out of retirement—your retirement why—is step one of retirement planning.

Goals and Purpose

I've counseled plenty of people whose retirement planning revolves around finances. I have to ask them, "What is the money for?" Some people come to me with a shopping list of things they want to do. Others haven't made a single goal for their retirement years—as if they stopped setting goals after they reached the pinnacle of their profession, or saved a certain amount of money, or moved into their dream home.

So why set goals in the first place? Humans are goal setters. It's in our nature. But there's a misconception about goals. They aren't meant to exist merely for the sake of achieving something. They exist to make us stretch, grow, push our limits, and expand our minds. This doesn't stop at a certain age. We're designed to grow during all life stages.

Retirement isn't meant to be a slow decline on the sofa. It's meant to be an opportunity to use that accumulated and hard-won experience and wisdom. And what a golden opportunity you have, now that you don't spend most of your waking hours working. When your life is less structured, and (hopefully) you're not living paycheck to paycheck and stressing about money, you can make a tremendous difference in your life, your family's lives, your community, and even the world.

For those who think that the point of retirement is to relax, to have zero responsibilities, and to only do what you want ... to a point, yes. I'm not here to judge your retirement choices (whatever you want to do, I'll help you finance it). I encourage you, however, to consider how fulfilled you'll be in these next several decades.

One study found that even if you are financially prepared for retirement, lacking goals may leave you feeling unsatisfied.[5]

Goals give you a reason to get up in the morning, and they don't have to be massive. You don't have to climb Mt. Everest. They can be as modest as cleaning the clutter out of the garage so you can actually park your car there. They can be moderately ambitious, like turning the garage into a woodworking shop or touring all of Scotland's ancient castles.

The beauty of retirement goals is that you can work on them whenever the spirit moves you, instead of squeezing them into your work schedule. Nobody is forcing you to set goals that don't resonate with you. The goals you set can move your life in the direction you want.

Many people slip into a comfortable and simple routine after retirement, and this period often centers on relaxation. Some people want to kick back and have nothing on the agenda for the foreseeable future. For a while, that's okay, if that's what you need. A rest period may be necessary.

But when you're rested and rejuvenated, then what? For most people, relaxation isn't sustainable. You can't sit by the pool for the rest of your life, as appealing as that may

---

5   Lifestyle Planning in the Transition to Retirement," *Journal of Aging Research and Lifestyle* 13 (2024): 30-32, https://doi.org/10.14283/jarlife.2024.4.

sound short term. At some point you'll have the itch to do something more stimulating. More meaningful.

A retirement without direction can quickly spiral into boredom. Boredom can have many negative effects, including poor mental health, physical health issues, and lower productivity levels.[6]

The main source of retirement angst is that it's hard to be happy if you have nothing to do and nowhere to begin. If you have a goal, at least you know what you can expect from the upcoming days. Otherwise, you're going through the motions—existing instead of living.

Please don't take this to mean that you should always be on the go, "doing, doing, doing." You also need to enjoy "being." There should be relaxation. There should be days when you choose to do nothing except leisurely flip through the pages of a book or enjoy your coffee on the deck and watch the clouds float by.

Another big reason retirees can experience anxiety and depression is a loss of sense of control over their lives. Have you ever noticed that when you're working toward a goal, it's like steering a ship toward a shore you want to visit? But when you're floating aimlessly with no goals in sight, the wind could blow you back to where you came from. Isn't it better to be at the helm deciding where you want to go?

---

6   Felix Miyago, "The Good and Bad of Boredom," *International Collegiate Journal of Science*, May 4, 2024, https://icjs.us/the-good-and-bad-of-boredom.

The Three Elements of Well-Being: The Retirement Trio

It is my opinion that a trio of elements come together to help one's well-being in retirement:

- Relationships
- Purpose
- Health

Can you imagine a happy retirement without all three? I think it would be incredibly empty. That's why I encourage people to set goals in all three areas.

What makes you happy? Volunteering? Traveling? Hanging out with the grandbabies to give your kids a break? A rich social life? Puttering around the house or tinkering in the garage? A hobby? Working part time? Creating?

Never think of your retirement years as "the end" or "the decline." They're called the golden years for a reason.

- Dame Judi Dench is a famous actress who didn't achieve fame until she was sixty-one.[7]
- Ray Kroc was fifty-nine when he purchased a small hamburger chain that later became McDonald's.[8]

7   Britannica, "Judi Dench," last updated April 19, 2025, https://www.britannica.com/biography/Judi-Dench.

8   Britannica, "Ray Kroc," last updated March 18, 2025, https://www.britannica.com/money/Ray-Kroc.

- Frank McCourt, bestselling author of *Angela's Ashes*, didn't start writing until he was sixty-five.[9]
- Yuichiro Miura climbed Mt. Everest in 2013, at age eighty.[10]
- Mohr Keet, World War II veteran, started bungee jumping at eighty-eight and became the world's oldest bungee jumper at ninety-six.[11]
- Karl Lagerfeld became head designer at Chanel at eighty-two.[12]
- Clara Peller (you'll remember her if you're "of a certain age") was eighty-one when she famously asked, "Where's the beef?" in a 1984 Wendy's commercial.[13]
- One study found that the average age of the most successful entrepreneurs is 45.[14]

9   Britannica, "Frank McCourt," last updated August 15, 2024, https://www.britannica.com/biography/Frank-McCourt-American-author.

10 "Oldest Person to Climb Everest (Male)," Guinness World Records, accessed May 30, 2025, https://www.guinnessworldrecords.com/world-records/oldest-person-to-climb-mt-everest-male#:~:text=The%20oldest%20man%20to%20ascend,of%2080%20years%20223%20days.

11 "Oldest Bungee Jumper," Guinness World Records, accessed May 30, 2025, https://www.guinnessworldrecords.com/world-records/oldest-bungee-jumper.

12 Tyler Piccotti et al., "Karl Lagerfeld," Biography.com, June 7, 2024, https://www.biography.com/history-culture/karl-lagerfeld.

13 Marc Berman, "'Where's The Beef'? The Iconic Clara Peller Spot For Wendy's Turns 40," Forbes, January 10, 2024, https://www.forbes.com/sites/marcberman1/2024/01/10/wheres-the-beef-the-iconic-clara-peller-spot-for-wendys-turns-40/

14 Benjamin F. Jones and Daniel Kim, "Most Successful Entrepreneurs Are Older Than You Think," Clifford-Lewis Private Wealth blog, February 11, 2023, https://www.clifford-lewis.com/blog/most-successful-entrepreneurs-are-older-than-you-think.

Whatever sparks your imagination, working toward that ideal can give your life purpose.

Even though having a purpose in life can lead to positive well-being, and research confirms this, I'm still surprised at how few people actually think about what would fulfill them in retirement.[15] I'm not here to tell you how you should live your retirement, but it's important for you to get clear on what you want and how you want to live your life. Don't just *think* about how you're going to fund your daily activities once you're no longer receiving a paycheck. Plan how you want to *feel* day-to-day: fulfilled and happy, with stimulating and meaningful things to do? Or frustrated and resentful, with no clear purpose?

It's important to discuss more than finances with your retirement planner. You need to also discuss the way you want to spend your precious time. Retirement (which, remember, is still a relatively new concept) is becoming more and more defined. It's no longer about "not working." A lot of people have objectives beyond not working. They may feel the urge to relocate to be closer to family, to participate in high-adrenaline pastimes, or to become involved in the community. You must ascertain what it means for you to retire on your terms.

Think about this, and think about it deeply: What are your plans for your time?

---

15   Louis Fang, Alfred Allan, and Joanne M. Dickson, "Purpose in Life and Associated Cognitive and Affective Mechanisms," Journal of Happiness Studies 25 (2024): 63, https://doi.org/10.1007/s10902-024-00771-6.

There is no right or wrong answer. Your response will influence the plan of how you're going to pay for the time you're not receiving a paycheck.

If you're stuck for ideas, let's look at the top three elements of a happy retirement.

According to social researchers, a quality retirement is composed of three elements: relationships (who you spend your time with), health (how you care for your body and mind), and core pursuits (how you spend your time).[16]

Relationships

Good relationships are the best predictors of happiness. Be sure to include goals that involve other people.

The ongoing Study of Adult Development shows without a shadow of a doubt that good relationships make for a happy life. The study began in 1938 with 268 male Harvard University sophomores who were deemed likely to succeed.[17] The study assessed various success indicators and was set up to track them for the next twenty years; however, the study didn't stop in 1958. It's still going on. Today, more than eighty years later, the study has expanded to over 450 men and includes inner-city Boston neighborhoods (men who have far less of a predicted chance to succeed). The study has also morphed from its original focus on success indicators

---

16   Jacob Schroeder, "How to Have a Happy Retirement," Kiplinger, December 30, 2024, https://www.kiplinger.com/retirement/happy-retirement/how-to-have-a-happy-retirement.

17   Study of Adult Development, Harvard University, accessed February 9, 2024, https://www.adultdevelopmentstudy.org/grantandglueckstudy.

to what is necessary to live a good life. Surprisingly, or not, happiness was not greater among the Harvard students with their historically higher professional accomplishments and net worth. Happiness was not tied to professional success. It was tied to one thing: love. George Vaillant, the study's leader for decades, said in 2012, "The only thing that really matters in life are your relationships to other people . . . Happiness equals love—full stop."[18]

How will you nurture relationships in retirement? List them now.

Health

As many people get older, they become more satisfied with their lives and stop seeking the elusive happiness of keeping up with the Joneses. Satisfaction, like good wine, tends to get better with age. Part of this depends on health.

Keeping healthy is a top priority for many retirees, especially given the astronomical cost of long-term health care. Rising health care expenses are at the top of many people's list of "Things to Worry about in Retirement" (we all have this list, whether it's on paper or in our heads).

Exercise, nutrition, healthy habits, and social connection are four ways you can prioritize your health. Whether you're healthy and want to keep it that way, motivated to course correct, or in poor health and have had a wake-up call, it's never too late to make improvements. As with finances,

---

18   George E. Valliant, *Triumphs of Experience: The Men of the Harvard Grant Study* (Cambridge, Massachusetts: Harvard University Press, 2012), https://doi.org/10.2307/j.ctt2jbxs1.

the sooner you start, the better. If you commit to your health today, you'll be on your way to a better tomorrow.

You can accomplish health goals and relationship goals together. Golf, hiking, cycling, dancing, tennis or pickleball, fitness classes, and martial arts are just a few ways to combine the social and physical elements of well-being. How will you improve or maintain your health? List them now.

Core Pursuits

Meaning and purpose come from your core pursuits, or what I call the "heart pursuits." What are you most passionate about?

Core pursuits are more than hobbies. They bring a sense of fulfillment and excitement—the kinds of activities you get lost in, where time ceases to exist, and you're in a wonderful state of flow.

You can have more than one core pursuit, and they don't have to cost money. The happiest people among my clients and acquaintances have four or more core interests. The unhappiest have two or fewer.

You can combine all three retirement goals: relationships, health, and core pursuits. Travel, volunteering, team or group sports, gardening clubs, and dance are a few examples of "all-in-one" activities.

One of the most powerful ways to achieve a sense of purpose is to think about others. To serve and to give. If your passion is painting, you wouldn't be nearly as satisfied with dozens of paintings stacked against the wall in your studio as you would be if you sold or gifted them to enrich other people's lives.

What would you love to do every day if money were no object? List them now.

What talents or gifts do you have that you could use to improve other people's lives? List them now.

I encourage you to think outside of what you think is possible for you. Dream! And then take time to write down four sets of goals:

- Daily (what you want your everyday life to look like)
- Short term (such as visiting the grandkids in another state)
- Mid term (such as turning the garage into a woodworking shop)
- Long term (such as traveling to every continent)

If you don't know what your ideal retirement is, you can't plan for it financially. That's step two.

Making Your Dreams Happen

One of the first questions I get asked is "Can I make my retirement dreams happen?" Once you've completed step one—knowing what you want out of retirement—we can sit down and look at funding those dreams while ensuring there's enough for basic needs and necessities.

I take a comprehensive approach. We can't talk about the money without talking about what it's going to be used for, and you can't plan what you want to do without knowing how to fund it. You may not have aspirations to travel the world, but even an easygoing backyard retirement with weekend barbecues and game nights with friends need to be planned for.

If people don't know what they're going to be doing beyond the first five or ten years of retirement, they could be in for a shock later on. Some want to continue enjoying an endless vacation—and believe me, that's incredibly appealing to most of us—but if they haven't set clear goals and budgeted for those goals, they could find themselves in the awful situation of having spent their retirement funds in five or ten years. And then what? How will they live? How will they manage if big health issues arise?

I'm not saying you can't squeeze every bit of juice out of your golden years—I highly recommend that you do. Just don't do it all at once. If you set goals, we must prioritize them and assess whether those goals are financially realistic. If you don't set goals, it's much harder to forecast the future and allocate your money wisely.

There's a flip side to this. Running out of money is a huge fear for many, so some people take their retirement strategy to the other extreme. They scrimp and save, stay cloistered at home, and miss out on a great retirement. We can talk about what you want to do in retirement, and about how much those things cost, so you can potentially avoid having excess money left over when you are gone. I also want to help you avoid deathbed regrets. You don't want to realize you wasted your retirement sitting in the backyard, too afraid to spend your money on things that made you feel alive when you actually had the means to travel the world while your body was still up for it.

You've worked hard your whole life. Your retirement is for you to enjoy, not to sit around and be bored so you have the "just-in-case" money. Our retirement plan will factor in your needs, of course, but also your heart's desires.

Whether you have a huge retirement nest egg or a peanut-sized one, you still need to know how you're going to spend your money (which funding "bucket" to allocate it to and later withdraw from).

I stress goal setting because the disbursement phase of your financial life (where you're no longer receiving a paycheck) can be hazardous. Many retirees simply don't factor in the delicate balance of the disbursement phase. The types of accounts you have, how much money you take out, which account you draw from, and when you draw from a certain account will have a big impact on how much taxes you pay and how long your money will last.

Without goals, you're in danger of making purchases on a whim, like buying a boat and putting expensive vacations on credit cards. You should spend your money as you see fit, of course, but as a retiree there are smart ways to pay for things and not-so-smart ways. And without having goals and knowing how those goals will be funded, retirees may end up resentful because they think they can't afford to have any fun. And they might be wrong.

I'm not telling you to plan out every single day of your retirement. That's impossible. But have an idea of what you want retirement to look like. Then we can determine your financial needs and ways to meet them today and long-term.

I like to ask my clients, "If money were no object, how would you like to spend your days? What would they look like?" Once that's clear, we can start thinking about funding those buckets and enjoying some perfect days.

Funding Your Goals and Dreams

For the most part, I've found that people are realistic about which dreams they can achieve in retirement. In fact, most people play it down. They think they don't have enough money to do anything really worthwhile.

After we've figured out how you're going to fund your everyday life, we can move on to the nice-to-haves, the dreams. I've seen it numerous times: When the must-haves are taken care of, retirees have more money than they thought for their nice-to-haves.

The ultimate happiness factor is to fund that first bucket, the liquidity bucket, that funds your immediate needs, all the way to the end of your retirement. Making sure your needs are taken care of helps to eliminate the daily stress and worry of wondering if you can pay your bills and still have enough left over to enjoy life. A lot of that has to do with when you start saving for retirement. A lot of people have big dreams. They want a memorable lifestyle when they retire, which is fantastic, but maybe they waited a long time to start saving. Starting too late can lead to a crushing reality check when you discover that certain goals are financially out of reach.

We can usually come up with alternatives that aren't quite as costly yet still deliver the same satisfaction. Whatever your dreams, whatever your financial starting point, we have to start by defining your goals.

The sooner you start, the more chances of success you have of fulfilling all your dreams. If you start younger and set those goals, you have something to work toward without hitting the panic button later on.

How young is "young"? Many of my clients come to me when they're in their forties and fifties. A lot of empty nesters experience a sudden wake-up call. The kids are gone, and the couple looks at each other and thinks, *Now what?* This often triggers introspection about the future, not just for the empty-nester chapter when they're still working but for the chapters that follow. It can be an exciting time.

Some clients come to me much later, on the brink of retirement. Ideally, you should start retirement planning in your thirties, but no matter your age, you need to start.

I don't want to make anyone feel ashamed for starting late. Some don't have a choice, and some simply didn't know that they were supposed to be making plans for the future, when the future seemed so far off. Suddenly, wham, the future is in their face. Let's start where you are and do the best we can.

If you wait to start planning until five years before retirement, you'll likely have less wiggle room to plan for the nicer parts of retirement. Some compromises may be warranted in terms of lifestyle and even standard of living, but honestly, we won't know that unless there are goals, or destinations, in place.

Talking about goals may seem like I'm talking about a bunch of intangibles.

What does "travel" mean anyway? Luxury five-star resort? Backpacking? Road trip? Cruise? Cabin on the lake? Six-week trips to the other side of the world? What does "purpose" mean? Accomplishing a dream? Being of service to others? Making the most of your talents?

A financial planner isn't supposed to talk about intangibles, right? But again, we have to look at what the money is for, because that will determine its disbursement amounts and timing. Setting goals in retirement is the first step in developing a plan to fund your needs and wants and to mitigate risks.

The Treasure Target

The Treasure Target is a handy chart that can help you understand how personal finance and goals go hand in hand. Developed by the Ron Blue Institute, an organization that teaches good financial stewardship, the Treasure Target defines the four core areas of financial life. I find it helpful when talking about core financial responsibilities and how that knowledge feeds into personal finance goals. The Treasure Target (and personal finance 101) will be covered more extensively in chapter 2.

TREASURE TARGET

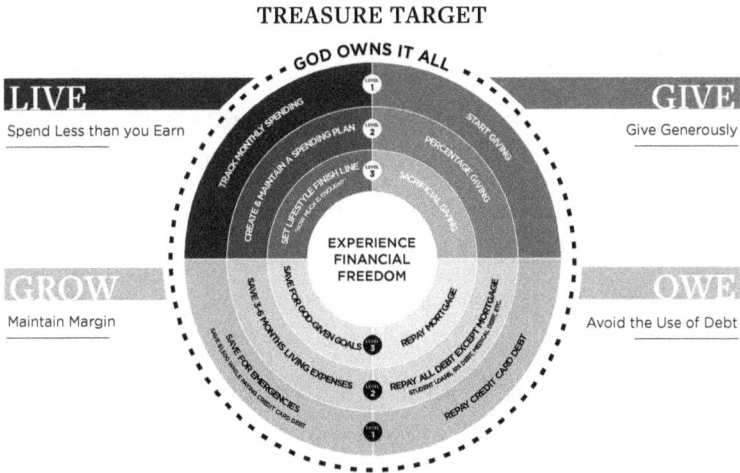

Source: Ron Blue Institute. Used by permission

Once you've defined your retirement goals, funding those goals is more than saying, "Save this much for this bucket and this much for that bucket." If you're not disciplined or you don't know the basics of personal finance, your chances of experiencing financial security go way down.

The Treasure Target is divided into four quadrants. Each quadrant helps to ensure that you have enough money for retirement in the way that you envision retirement to be. We begin on the outer rings of the circle and move inward. This gives you an idea of what the priorities are in each quadrant.

At the center, once we've gone through the rings of each quadrant, you can experience financial freedom— knowing that you've been disciplined and strategic with your money so that you have enough to last and enough to fund a retirement you will enjoy.

The "give" quadrant usually causes the most stress for people. If you're one of the millions of Americans who don't have enough saved for retirement, charitable giving may seem out of the realm of possibility. Giving is an essential part of happiness, but how can you justify giving money you don't have? Let me put your mind at ease. You don't have to give money. Many retirees find their "soul purpose" through volunteering. Imagine if you gave 10 percent of your extra time to an organization or cause you care about.

But let's not get ahead of ourselves. The point of this chapter is to help you define, or refine, how you expect your retirement to look: day-to-day, the next few years, the next few decades.

Your personal finance plan should help protect you from the unexpected, mitigate risk, and allow you to get the most out of this time.

Start Here, Now

According to the Centers for Disease Control and Prevention, today's average lifespan is 79.1 years for women and 73.2 years for men (a combined average of 76 in the

United States).[19] In 2019, the average lifespan was closer to 80, but the pandemic took some people before their time and skewed the numbers. Now, I predict the average life expectancy to grow once more. This means you'll likely need to plan for at least two decades, if not three, as a retiree.

Here's how to get started:

1. Determine your relationship, health, and core pursuit goals.
2. Plan for your short-term needs. Calculate your current and then your anticipated expenses in retirement.
3. Carve out enough cash to meet your retirement needs for the next two to three years. Set that money aside in the first funding bucket, the liquidity bucket that will meet your immediate needs including basic expenses. Once you are assured you have enough to live on, we can look at the future and explore discretionary spending.

Having enough saved for the future can help alleviate some of the stress of not knowing how tomorrow will pan out. It's a start, but we still have a long way to go.

---

19   National Center for Health Statistics, "Life Expectancy in the U.S. Dropped for the Second Year in a Row in 2021," Centers for Disease Control and Prevention, August 31, 2022, https://www.cdc.gov/nchs/pressroom/nchs_press_releases/2022/20220831.htm.

There's no getting around knowing how to manage your money. And that takes discipline.

———

CHAPTER 2

———

Personal Finance 101

I mentioned that many of my clients are not well versed in personal finance. Finance is not something we're taught in school, and so I find that people continually make mistakes that affect their lifestyles now and in the future. This chapter will change all that. It may give you the foundation for taking control of your personal finances. It will help you become financially independent, whether you're in your working years or retired.

We'll start with the Treasure Target that was introduced in chapter 1 and then move on to the Four Hs of Financial Wisdom as developed by the Ron Blue Institute.

These graphics condense what you'll need to know to help you reach financial independence. You'll learn the importance of tracking expenses, budgeting, managing debt, and saving. We'll discuss something that many people overlook in their everyday finances: opportunity cost.

This chapter is the foundation of personal finance for retirement. Even if you've been successful at managing your finances, this chapter could open your eyes to a new way of looking at money.

I also want to preface this section by saying you must have these core principles in place before we start planning your retirement. There's no getting around knowing how to manage your money. And that takes discipline. Managing your money is a way to show yourself some love. You're doing this for you. The hardest part is starting. Once you're used to it, it's easy to continue.

The Treasure Target

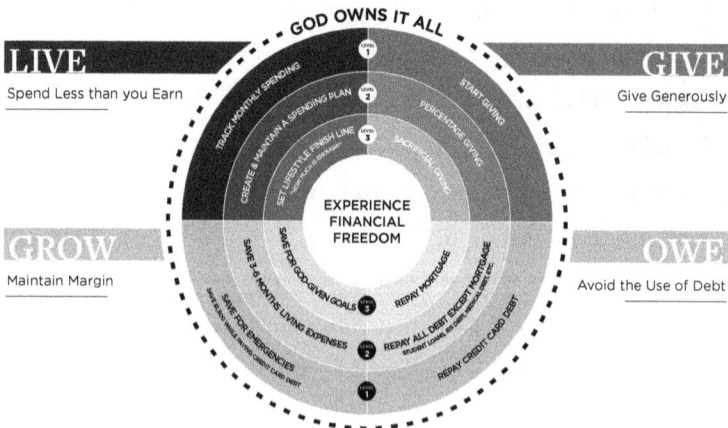

The Treasure Target is laid out in a circle with concentric rings of different levels and four quadrants. We start at the outermost ring and work our way into the center, where you can "experience financial freedom." It's important to note that you don't have to finish all of ring one (or level one) before you move on to ring two. You could be in ring one in Live and Give, ring two in Grow, and ring three in Owe. Everybody's different, and it's not necessarily a linear journey to the center. You'll likely need to make sacrifices in some areas to move ahead in others. But eventually, if you keep going, you'll reach the Treasure Target in the center.

In the outermost circle, we see "God owns it all." The point here is that it's important to be a good steward of your money, to respect and to be grateful for what you've been provisioned.

Live

We begin with the "Live" quadrant because this represents the money you need to survive. Whatever your financial situation at retirement, you must have enough to live on. The main principle here is to spend less than you earn.

Many people of all financial walks of life don't track their monthly spending. That's where we begin, on level one. Yes, tracking expenses can be tedious, but it's worth it because a lot of people have only a vague idea where their money is going—and they're often shocked when they see how much their discretionary spending habits sabotage their future financial security. Even people who have a budget don't necessarily track their spending, so their budget could be completely unrealistic. This can be a rude awakening.

I recommend that you track your spending for a minimum of three to six months. I find a lot of people get in the habit of tracking spending and then end up continuing to do it. There are some great apps you can use to track spending on the go. Or you can use a spreadsheet, a tracking tool provided by your bank, or even a checkbook-style log. Whatever works for you. Just do it.

Tracking expenses for three to six months forces you to look where your money is going. When I say track spending, I'm talking about tracking *everything*. You might not realize you spend fifty dollars a week on coffee. You might find that you have a monthly automatic renewal subscription you forgot about, or you have four streaming services on autopay. Autopay is convenient, but if you forget that you have it, those payments can add up fast. The discretionary autopay subscriptions and the impulse spending habits kill us financially.

Don't look at tracking and budgeting as restrictive handcuffs. It can actually be the opposite. It can be freeing because you know exactly where your money is going. If you have to cut back in one area, you know exactly where you can cut back and where to allocate that "newfound" money. You can still spend fifty bucks a week on coffee if that's a choice you make and as long as you're okay with that amount. It's shocking sometimes how much we spend at the grocery store, for example. We've all gone shopping hungry or without a list and end up purchasing five thousand extra things.

Impulse buying tempts us all. We love shiny things! People with marketing degrees know to place certain things in front of us in a particular way to play on our psyches. They know exactly what buttons to push to get us to impulse buy something. Marketers play on our discretionary spending, and most of us aren't immune to their tactics. That's why tracking is so critical.

So again, the first level is to track your monthly spending—know where your money is going. You can't budget, you can't plan, and you can't make adjustments unless you know what's going on.

Level two is to create and maintain a spending plan, or a realistic budget. Tracking and budgeting go hand in hand, but you have to start tracking first before you can solidify a budget.

Your budget will evolve as you go through this tracking exercise. It's a living, breathing document, especially the first three, six, or nine months. Expect that your budget will change based on the hard data that comes from tracking your spending. Once you get into a routine, you'll find it's easier to make better spending choices and big-picture financial decisions.

Your success rate of saving and getting to where you want to be in retirement goes way up if you have these core principles in place. If you don't track and budget, your success rate goes down.

After tracking, we move into budgeting. A budget is created based on data that comes from tracking. The budget *must* be based on what you found on your tracking. I like to call it zero-dollar budgeting. Every dollar should be accounted for, and your remaining dollars should be zero. This isn't to say that you should spend every single penny. Not at all. It means every single penny is accounted for. That could mean some of your money is going to savings, some to education funds or retirement funds, or some to fun, but you know exactly where it's going. You're accounting for *everything*, and then later in the process you create a discretionary (wants and nice-to-haves) fund for those coffees and indulgences that you would like to enjoy as a retiree.

Tracking enables you to plan for a reasonable budget and make adjustments. That's the key. Once you put this together, you may realize you're not putting enough into retirement. Or you're not putting enough into your kids' education fund or your vacation fund. But now you have some hard data that helps you identify where you can adjust. Where can you sacrifice or put off? What can you get rid of?

Tracking and budgeting may prevent getting into the last-minute "oh crap" scenario of having to rob Peter to pay Paul because you don't have any other options.

After you establish that budget, the key is maintaining it. Sure, you'll make adjustments as life happens and your financial needs change, but maintaining a budget and creating a lifestyle around what you have, not what you're hoping to have, will lead to financial independence.

I want to highlight this: As you're setting your lifestyle and your spending plan, always pause before you make big purchases. Think about this potential purchase. Do you really need this? Do you really need this *now*? Don't give in to impulse buying. Set a threshold of anything over a certain dollar value, pause, and ask yourself, "Is this worth it?"

Anything you buy has what's called *opportunity cost*. Whatever you spend money on is at the expense of something else that you could or need to spend money on. This will be critical through retirement when you're not bringing home a paycheck.

Ask yourself these questions: What's the opportunity cost of making that purchase or making this decision? If I do this now, what won't I be able to do later? If I do this now, am I going to have the retirement I want? If I do this now, am I going to be able to pay for my kids' college? Is it worth it to enjoy this now if it means putting off that vacation I want to take?

When you're mindful of the opportunity cost, your success rate of saving and living within your means can go way up.

The next ring, level three, in the "Live" quadrant of the Treasure Target is the "set lifestyle finish line." How much money is enough? That's different for everybody. Again, no judgment. Some people are used to living on a shoestring, while others live a more luxurious lifestyle. You set your lifestyle based on your end goal. What does your monthly budget need to look like to give yourself a sense of security while still working toward your goals?

Level three also asks "How much is enough?" This refers to your priorities. How much do you want to put toward all your different categories? How much do you want to put toward retirement? How much do you want to put toward savings for education, vacation, or other big purchases? How much are you going to put toward helping others and giving?

As we go through the other quadrants, once again your budget will be refined. How much are you going to give? How much are you going to invest? How much debt will you pay off? Our goal here is to create a margin, a buffer, an excess in your budget.

Everybody has their own ideal number when it comes to feeling secure about finances. It's not a one size fits all. When we're applying Biblical principles, I always tell people that, yes, God owns it all, but He never said He doesn't want us to have money or enjoy life. God never said it's better to be poor.

Give

Let's talk about generosity in the "Give" quadrant.

Ask yourself, "Am I worshiping money, or am I worshiping *with* money?"

He did say to be generous. Generosity is key to being good stewards of what we have. There are plenty of examples of people giving everything away. The point is not what others do, but what are *you* doing with *your* money? God wants us to have happiness and joy, but He also counsels us to be aware of whether we are loving: money or loving what we can do with money. Are we worshiping wealth or are we worshiping *with* our wealth?

If you worship money, then it's all about you. If you worship with your wealth, then you could be living your life while also helping others. We're all called on this earth for a reason. We all have a purpose in life, specific talents that make it "easy" for us to do things that others find difficult. If we're financially responsible, we're often better able to fulfill God's plan for us. If we don't follow the principles that are laid before us and are not able to do what He's asked us to do, then that's a fail. We're not fulfilling our purpose because we're so focused on survival.

Tracking, budgeting, and setting the lifestyle are the core of the Live quadrant where we make sure our everyday needs are met and there's something left over so we can fulfill our higher purpose in the Give quadrant.

As much as you can, give generously. You have to start somewhere in that outer ring, in level one. Start giving what you can so you get into the giving mindset.

The Bible says that God always likes a cheerful giver, not a begrudging giver. The tithe is the only place in the

Bible He says to test Him in this . . . the blessing will pour out. Of course, we're not all financially at the point where there's a lot of extra money to give sacrificially, so we need to work our way to build a margin, to be able to give more. Once you have your budget set—and giving should be part of your budget—you factor in a giving portion.

The reasons to give are partly because it's a Biblical principle. Another is that from a human mindset standpoint, joy comes inherently to us when we help other people. Whether or not you're that type of person, when we help somebody, we feel better. We feel a sense of deep happiness. It's in our DNA to be generous. And in this way, giving helps in the retirement happy factor.

Start giving and step your way into level two, percentage giving. That's the tithe piece where you give, say, 10 percent of your income. Level three is sacrificial giving, where you've refined your budget and gotten out of debt, and you now have the margin to start giving above and beyond a basic tithe. You're giving out of the generosity of your heart. You want to, and you're able to. That's fantastic.

Owe

The next quadrant is Owe, which focuses on avoiding and eliminating debt.

There's good debt and there's bad debt. Avoiding debt really means avoiding bad debt such as credit cards. Obviously, the goal would be to get out of debt 100 percent, but that's hard to do in this day and age. As with everything, you have to start somewhere. But if you budget properly, and you're aware of opportunity cost, you're less likely to whip out the credit card, make an impulse buy, and stay stuck in debt.

Always think about the opportunity cost of credit cards. Are you able to get out of debt? Are you able to save the way you need to? To get out of debt, let's face it, you must make sacrifices. It's not a fun thing, but to get to that inner circle of financial freedom and to have a higher success rate for retirement, you have to get out of debt.

With the interest rates that credit card companies charge, which are upward of 25–30 percent, how are you ever going to make that up in savings or investments? Even if you're making a 10 percent return on a stock market investment, you're still paying 15–20 percent to that credit card bank. That doesn't make sense. You're going backward, giving your money to the bank. So why don't we just eliminate that bank?

You simply can't get ahead when you're paying high interest rates. It's impossible.

A lot of people are forced to go into debt when they're young, when they get divorced, or when there's a crisis of some sort. It's great if people don't get into debt, but most do, and it seems like an inevitable part of life these days. Thinking ahead to retirement, however, you *must* commit to finding a way out. Otherwise, that debt will get bigger and bigger, and it will become less and less possible to live a financially stable retirement. Think of it this way: As a new retiree, do you want to be making payments on a vacation or the expensive furniture you bought ten years ago? No! You want those things paid off in full so you can stop giving your hard-earned money to creditors.

Now granted, some people are in circumstances where they can't get out of debt, at least not in the immediate future. But by putting some of these principles in place and changing their mindset, they can work their way toward being debt free. Every little bit helps.

You have to look long term. It's all about the opportunity cost. You either choose to sacrifice now for more fulfillment and happiness down the road or be burdened with the fallout from a big purchase (or a lot of small, seemingly insignificant purchases) for the rest of your life.

Another thing to keep in mind is that nearly everything you buy continues to "charge" you in the form of rent because you have to put your stuff somewhere, you have to have insurance to protect it, and you have to maintain it. Those costs add up, so it's worthwhile considering them as part of the opportunity cost of the items you want to purchase. The lifetime cost of even the little stuff adds up fast too.

Credit card debt traps you. The only way to freedom is to get rid of credit cards. You can keep one credit card to maintain your credit score and for emergencies or rewards, but you must commit to paying it off monthly. If you're not disciplined enough or you're unable to pay the balance every month, don't use it. It's not worth it.

How do you accomplish level one of the Owe quadrant, to repay credit card debt?

Start with store credit cards. Pay them off and get rid of them. Then use the snowball method: Pay the balances of any credit cards where you can afford to pay off the principal. Once those are paid off, you apply the amounts you formerly paid into the small balances into the bigger balances.

Paying the smallest debt first is a rewarding way to pay off credit card debt. It may sound counterintuitive, but paying the smallest debt first doesn't necessarily mean paying the one with the highest interest rate. Pay the one with the smallest balance. Continue to make minimum payments on the cards with bigger balances, but prioritize getting rid of the card with the smallest balance. Then cut it up. Paying off one card is a huge mental win that will encourage you to keep going until you've paid off every card.

Gradually chipping away at your credit card debt is incredibly liberating.

You may feel the urge to get rid of the biggest balance first, but that's usually impossible. You can't go after the biggest balance because the minimum payments are big, and paying minimums never makes the balance disappear. If you can't pay off the principal, you could be stuck forever.

Human nature loves these small victories. Each paid-off, cut-up card is a triumph. You celebrate, and you tackle the next one. I've found that the snowball method has a greater success rate than other methods because of the wins along the way. You're more likely to stick with it instead of giving up when faced with those ugly balances.

Case Study: Mila

After Mila got divorced, she lived off her credit cards for a long time. She wasn't getting spousal support (the couple had agreed that Mila's husband would pay for college in lieu of spousal support), and she was working minimum-wage jobs. Mila had been a stay-at-home mom and was new to the job market after fifteen years. Until she got a better-paying and higher-skilled job, she was putting everything on credit cards—her food, gas, and utilities, which all quickly added up to the tune of $35,000 in credit card debt.

As soon as Mila was able, she began chipping away at the credit card debt using the snowball method.

It wasn't an easy road to eliminate the burden of this debt. Mila often wondered how she was going to make it until her next paycheck. "In the beginning it was like, okay, how am I going to make it through the week with three bucks in my account?" she said. "And then I'd look at my fridge and pantry and see enough food for two weeks, and there was a little gas in the car. Okay, deep breath. I'm good. I don't have to go anywhere except work, and I don't need to buy anything. I'm good until next payday."

She quickly learned how to say no to impulse buys and any discretionary spending that didn't enrich her life in some way.

It took a little more than a decade for Mila to pay off her credit cards. As soon as she paid one off, she cut it up, until she was left with one credit card for emergencies. This disciplined approach taught her to live 100 percent within her means. She hasn't used credit since. Her next objective is to pay off her house while also putting enough away for her emergency fund.

Mila is now an American anomaly: As she approaches retirement, she is 100 percent debt free. She doesn't have any savings beyond her emergency fund, but she's poised to fast-track her retirement savings without the worry of carrying any debt into retirement.

When I heard Mila's story, I thought, *She's investing in herself.* Mila invested in her future by putting the Financial Planning 101 principles in place. Even if you don't think you're as disciplined as our case study example, you can become so. It just takes discernment when you're shopping— and a choice to stop being so generous to the banks. That money you're paying in interest, keep it for yourself.

After you get rid of your credit card debt, move your way into level two, paying all other debts, like student loans, IRS debt, car loans, and medical bills.

The last level of Owe is to repay your mortgage. People often ask me, "Do I repay my mortgage before I get into retirement, or should I leave it?" Your mortgage is the last thing you pay off because generally it has much lower interest rates than other debt. You also get tax deductions if you have a mortgage. Some people will say, "I won't get my tax deduction if I pay off my mortgage," but I ask them whether their tax deduction is less than the amount they pay the lender. In most cases the tax deduction is nowhere near big enough to justify keeping a mortgage payment.

Paying off a mortgage early or leveraging the equity in the home is a case-by-case situation that should be discussed with a financial planner. For now I want to emphasize the importance of being as debt free as you can as you enter retirement.

Any way you slice it, if you can avoid paying *any* kind of interest rates, whether it's "good debt" or "bad debt," do it. That's money you can save, invest, give, or play with. Speaking of giving—don't be generous with your money when it comes to paying interest to the banks. Think of the wonderful things you could do with 25 percent annual interest of the $7,951 that the average American owed on credit cards in 2024.[20]

The ultimate goal is to be mortgage free in retirement because that takes a huge expense off the table. Being mortgage free will give you more leeway in retirement. Not everybody gets to the third level of the Owe quadrant, but it's a good goal to aim for. If you're carrying your mortgage into retirement, you may want to clear all your other debt before you retire, if at all possible.

---

20   Angelica Leicht, "Here's How Much Credit Card Debt the Average American Has (and How to Pay It Off)," CBS News, April 26, 2024, https://www.cbsnews.com/news/heres-how-much-credit-card-debt-the-average-american-has-and-how-to-pay-it-off.

Grow

The last quadrant of the Treasure Target is Grow. The Grow section focuses on two different levels of emergency funds. These are critical safety nets that most people don't have—and they're essential in retirement.

The first emergency fund is for short-term emergencies like your car breaking down, veterinarian bills, appliance repair, or a leaking roof. This could be $1,000 or whatever cash you feel comfortable having on hand when life throws you a monkey wrench. The only caveat is that you must replenish it every time you use it.

Building up emergency reserves will likely slow down the rate at which you repay debt, but it serves the principle of paying yourself first so that you can survive without relying on credit cards and their expensive interest rates. Using an emergency fund is still cheaper overall than putting an emergency car repair on a credit card if you can't pay that credit card bill immediately.

The second emergency fund is more long term: Having enough money to live on for at least six months. I recommend saving up six months of living expenses, at a minimum, and more if you're able, so you don't have to rely on credit cards when you're most vulnerable. As a retiree, when you're not receiving a regular paycheck, or if you've been laid off or disabled, your retirement income may not be sufficient to pay off the debt of a 29 percent annual percentage rate credit card. If something catastrophic happens, heaven forbid, you'll have confidence knowing this safety net is there.

Once your immediate survival needs are taken care of and you have adequate emergency funds, it's time to focus on your retirement goals. Whatever you want to do with your life is probably going to take money. Maybe you want to take a dream vacation, or you want to help pay for your grandkids' education, or you want to contribute to a cause you're passionate about. The goal is to have enough for a happy retirement, however you define it.

This goes back to what we talked about in chapter 1. What do you want to do in retirement? What's your purpose? What do you want your everyday life to look like? What's going to make you happy? The chances of you having a fulfilling retirement can increase dramatically if you can get to that third rung of the Treasure Target. You have to be able to fund that.

Believe me, I'm not tying money to happiness. We're defining what your goals are first, and then we're figuring out how we enable you to live out those goals.

Where and how does money help facilitate a happy retirement? It's hard to give your all to a noble cause, or to fulfill your destiny, if all you can think about is how you're going to keep a roof over your head.

We've discussed the four quadrants of the Treasure Target. Now let's move on to the Four Hs of Financial Wisdom. They're similar to the Treasure Target, but the four Hs look at your finances from a different angle.

The Four Hs of Financial Wisdom

The Four Hs of Financial Wisdom delve into the intangibles of finance. These tools are a heart-centered, personal approach that speaks to the emotions of retirement rather than the hard facts and figures of the Treasure Target. The four Hs and the Treasure Target both help you achieve the same goal of financial independence.

The Four Hs of Financial Wisdom:

- Heart: Behavior follows belief
- Health: The reality of today's finances
- Habits: The five Biblical principles of money
- Hope: The promise of tomorrow

THE FOUR Hs OF FINANCIAL WISDOM

HEART: BEHAVIOR FOLLOWS BELIEF

Stewardship
Psalm 24:1

Contentment
Philippians 4:11-13;
Hebrews 13:5

Faith
Hebrews 11:1,6

Wisdom
James 3:16-17;
James 1:5

Stewardship: Do I believe that God owns it all?

Contentment: Do I believe that what I have right now is enough?

Faith: Do I believe that I demonstrate my faith through my finances?

Wisdom: Do I believe that God's wisdom is true and available?

HEALTH: TODAY'S REALITY

There are five simultaneous competing priorities for the use of money. God's Word speaks to each:

Live
Give
GOD OWNS IT ALL
Owe (TAXES)
Owe (DEBT)
Grow

Live: Practice care, contentment, and celebration because money is a tool. (Acts 4:34-35; 1 Timothy 6:8, 6:17; Hebrews 11:24-26)

Give: Open my hand to release God's resources. He wants my heart connected to His Kingdom story. (Matthew 6:19-24; 2 Corinthians 9:6-8; Luke 16:13)

Owe (Debt): Eliminate debt because debt always presumes upon the future. (Proverbs 22:7; James 4:13-16)

Owe (Taxes): Pay taxes with gratitude. They reflect God's provision. (Matthew 22:17-21)

Grow: Demonstrate financial maturity by giving up today's desires for tomorrow's benefit. (Proverbs 6:6-8; Luke 12:16-21)

HABITS: FIVE BIBLICAL PRINCIPLES

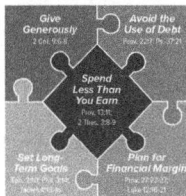

Give Generously
2 Cor. 9:6-8

Avoid the Use of Debt
Prov. 22:7; Ps. 37:21

Spend Less Than You Earn
Prov. 13:11;
2 Thes. 3:6-9

Set Long-Term Goals

Plan for Financial Margin
Prov. 27:23-27;
Luke 12:16-21

RON BLUE INSTITUTE

HOPE: TOMORROW'S PROMISE

Changing habits to increase margin is the only way to meet long-term goals and align our hearts and hope toward eternity.

Stable
"Saving some with an emergency fund"

Surviving
"Living paycheck to paycheck"

Secure
"Saving for long-term goals"

Struggling
"Not able to make ends meet"

Margin Meter

Surplus
"More than enough"

Source: Ron Blue Institute. Used with permission.

Heart

HEART: BEHAVIOR FOLLOWS BELIEF

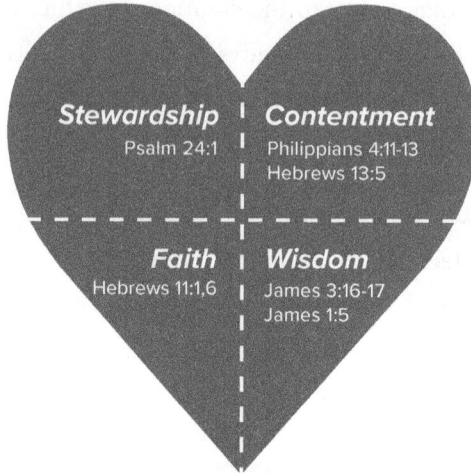

Stewardship
Psalm 24:1

Contentment
Philippians 4:11-13
Hebrews 13:5

Faith
Hebrews 11:1,6

Wisdom
James 3:16-17
James 1:5

Stewardship: Do I believe that God owns it all?

Contentment: Do I believe that what I have right now is enough?

Faith: Do I believe that I demonstrate my faith through my finances?

Wisdom: Do I believe that God's wisdom is true and available?

"Behavior follows belief" refers to your attitude about money.

We break the heart into four different quadrants of stewardship, contentment, faith, and wisdom.

First quadrant, stewardship: Do we believe God owns it all? Are we being good stewards of what we've been given? Is good stewardship in our hearts? If you don't share those beliefs, you can still ask yourself whether you're a good steward of the money you've worked so hard for.

Second quadrant, contentment. Do we believe that what we have right now is enough? Are we grateful for what we have, even if it's not exactly where we would like to be? Are we in a place of contentment? And if not, how do we get there?

Third quadrant, faith. How do we demonstrate our faith through finances? Are we worshiping wealth, or are we worshiping *with* our wealth?

Fourth quadrant, wisdom. This once again ties into stewardship, which can be tied into ancient principles. There are over two thousand verses in the Bible that talk about money stewardship, and those principles still apply today.

Email Support@RetireWisePro.com if you would like a free worksheet on the Four Hs of Financial Wisdom. It's an incredibly handy self-analysis that helps you get clear on your finances.

Health

HEALTH: TODAY'S REALITY

There are five simultaneous competing priorities for the use of money. God's Word speaks to each:

Live: Practice care, contentment, and celebration because money is a tool. (Acts 4:34-35; 1 Timothy 6:8, 6:17; Hebrews 11:24-26)

Give: Open my hand to release God's resources. He wants my heart connected to His Kingdom story. (Matthew 6:19-24; 2 Corinthians 9:6-8; Luke 16:13)

Owe (Debt): Eliminate debt because debt always presumes upon the future. (Proverbs 22:7; James 4:13-16)

Owe (Taxes): Pay taxes with gratitude. They reflect God's provision. (Matthew 22:17-21)

Grow: Demonstrate financial maturity by giving up today's desires for tomorrow's benefit. (Proverbs 6:6-8; Luke 12:16-21)

You'll recognize the elements of financial health: live, give, owe, and grow. In this case Owe is broken down into debt and taxes to add another perspective.

The health graphic reiterates that there will be simultaneous and competing priorities for your money: savings, debt payoff, living expenses. We have to balance the needs of the Live, Give, Owe, and Grow quadrants. If you tie these into your retirement goals, you can prioritize spending.

It's important to see money as a tool, not a master. Get into the right mindset of feeling financially abundant. Open your hands. Open your heart to give and unlock that happiness. Unlock what the joy of giving could bring, not only to you but to others. And start having that mindset to live in a place of margin so that you can give.

Gratitude plays a big part in your financial health, too, because it's tied to your psychological health. We love to complain about taxes, for example, but we have to remember we receive services for those taxes. We may disagree on how much we pay in taxes, but think of it as a provision. We go to a store, or a hairdresser, or an auto mechanic, and we pay them for services. The same can be said for our tax money. We get benefits like police, fire, roads, and schools. We can vote certain ways to influence how our tax money is spent, but above all, gratitude will help put things into perspective.

Growing your money demonstrates financial maturity. You give up today's desires for tomorrow's benefit. There's that opportunity cost again. I'm not saying "Don't have fun today!" Absolutely not. Enjoy life. Have fun. But be smart about it. There's a balance. Be thinking of your future too. Think about how many years you're going to spend in retirement. A decade? Two decades? Three? More? You've worked hard your whole life, so you deserve to enjoy your retirement. It doesn't matter if you're sitting on the couch relaxing or helping ten thousand charities. You earned it. Enjoy it. Today's financial decisions can help to enable a financially confident tomorrow.

Habits

HABITS: FIVE BIBLICAL PRINCIPLES

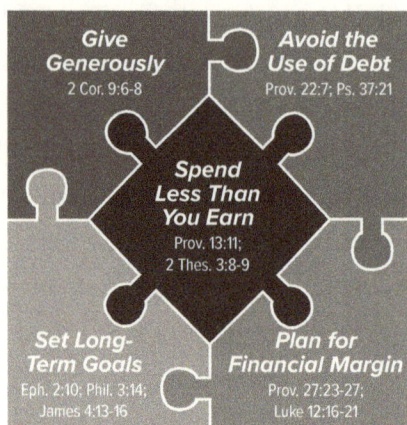

Give Generously
2 Cor. 9:6-8

Avoid the Use of Debt
Prov. 22:7; Ps. 37:21

Spend Less Than You Earn
Prov. 13:11; 2 Thes. 3:8-9

Set Long-Term Goals
Eph. 2:10; Phil. 3:14; James 4:13-16

Plan for Financial Margin
Prov. 27:23-27; Luke 12:16-21

Habits are how you manage your money day in and day out. Do you consciously avoid debt? Do you set long-term goals? Do you plan and take steps to achieve financial margin? Do you tend to impulse shop, or do you weigh the opportunity cost of every purchase? Do you save and invest for your future? Do you give generously?

At the center of this is the wise counsel of the ages: Spend less than you earn. Developing better financial habits will be at the core of achieving the Treasure Target, which can lead to financial stability during retirement.

Hope

HOPE: TOMORROW'S PROMISE

Changing habits to increase margin is the only way to meet long-term goals and align our hearts and hope toward eternity.

Stable
"Saving some with an emergency fund"

Surviving
"Living paycheck to paycheck"

Secure
"Saving for long-term goals"

Struggling
"Not able to make ends meet"

Margin Meter

Surplus
"More than enough"

In the Hope quadrant, we're focused on tomorrow's promise, which means changing our habits to increase margin. Moving the "margin meter" from struggling to surplus is the only way to meet long-term goals and align our hearts and hopes toward the future and toward God's plan. Are you aligning today's spending with what you want tomorrow? It's difficult to respond to God's call without a margin. It's difficult to give without a margin. It's difficult to make it through a three decade–long retirement without budgeting. If you don't have a margin, your chances of success in setting and achieving any financial goal are slim to none.

The Four Hs of Financial Wisdom worksheet has a great little metric that asks where you are financially right now. Are you struggling? Can you make ends meet? Are you living paycheck to paycheck? Are you stable? Do you have an emergency fund? Are you secure? Or are you all the way over to surplus where you have a ton of margin? Where are your gauges for what makes a comfortable lifestyle? How much do you need every month to feel secure? It's different for everybody, but it's a good indicator. It's a good visual.

Knowing where you are now is the first step to putting the throttle down, pedal to the metal, to get all the way over to the margin side of that meter.

These core principles are tools to get you thinking about your financial heart, health, habits, and hope. They illuminate how you're approaching your finances. They show you whether you're being honest with yourself, and they show you exactly where you are in these different segments.

Above all, be honest with yourself as you begin your journey toward financial security in retirement. Use the four Hs as an assessment tool to see where your heart is, where your mindset is, and where your weaknesses lie. The worksheet will help you identify your weak spots if you're honest with yourself.

Once you identify your weak spots, then you know where you can put some of the attention and lay the groundwork so you can move to the next phase of putting the plan in action. You won't have a chance at being success-ful without a plan. Financial plans will not have the positive effects on your saving unless you are honest with yourself and stick to the guidelines you have established.

The whole point of the Treasure Target and the Four Hs of Financial Wisdom is to get you to stop and evaluate how you are with money. You have to do this honestly and nonjudgmentally. Once you have the core principles in place, you'll feel empowered and confident to move to the next phase.

In this chapter you've learned the basics of personal finance. The Treasure Target and the Four Hs of Financial Wisdom are the foundation for financial independence in retirement. In the next section, we'll discuss funding strategies: where to put your money in each phase of retirement.

As we embark into retirement planning, we need to keep in mind that both the accumulation phase and the distribution/drawdown phase are equally important to a successful retirement plan. We also need to introduce protection strategies for your nest egg during critical times.

The following graphic depicts the full journey we're going to discuss in Section 2: The Retire Happy Framework™.

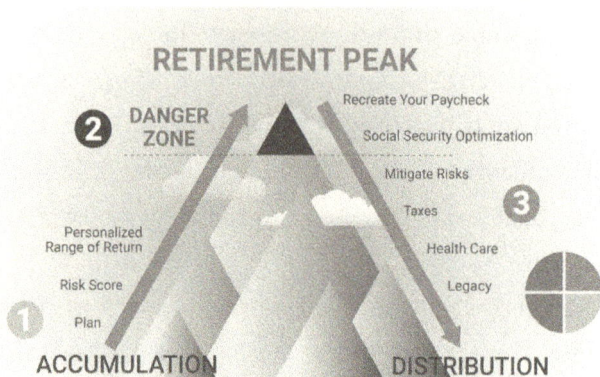

RETIREMENT PEAK

DANGER ZONE ②

③

Recreate Your Paycheck
Social Security Optimization
Mitigate Risks
Taxes
Health Care
Legacy

Personalized Range of Return
Risk Score
Plan ①

ACCUMULATION   **DISTRIBUTION**

Phase 1 GROW	Phase 2 PRESERVE	Phase 3 SPEND
The purpose is to accumulate wealth and the primary risk is market volatility.	This is the pre-retirement years. The primary purpose is to still grow, but prevent a catastrophic loss to your nest egg. The primary risk we are solving for is loss.	The purpose is to recreate your paycheck with social security, and your wealth with out running out of money. The primary risk we are solving for is longevity risk and sequence of return risk.

Source: Retire Wise, LLC

This graphic illustrates a key point: The downhill journey, when you're no longer collecting a paycheck, can be fraught with dangers. The Retire Happy Framework™ will help you navigate this journey safely.

SECTION 2

———

The Retire Happy Framework™

Section 2 outlines the reality of the retirement planning journey and how to start planning. At this point, you've identified what you want your retirement to look like. You've been introduced to the foundational principles of finance that I adhere to. Now it's time to put it all together.

This is where The Retire Happy Framework™ comes in to help make your confidence in retirement a priority and a reality. We have to account for risks, build a plan to address those risks, and structure the funding and drawdown phase the proper way to help ensure your needs are met and you have enough money to live well.

With a plan, it's possible to live your version of a happy retirement. Chapter 3 will discuss the risks associated with retirement. We've already discussed your ideal retirement, and chapter 3 will look at what could get in the way financially.

To guide us through this section, we'll dissect the "three sets of threes," which refer to several ways of looking at what your money is for and ways to fund your retirement.

The first set involves the three phases of retirement: the Go-Go Years (the first few years of retirement), the Slow-Go Years (the mid years of retirement when you begin to slow down), and the No-Go Years (the last years of your retirement when you almost completely cease activity). Each phase contains aspects from the next two sets of three, and each has a different funding and disbursement strategy. We'll discuss these phases of retirement in chapter 4.

The second set involves your needs, wants, and wishes in retirement. These identify where the money is going. Needs, wants, and wishes are slightly different in each phase of retirement. These categories will be discussed as they pertain to each stage of retirement.

The third set involves the three funding buckets: where the money is being placed for immediate use (the liquidity bucket), where it's being placed for growth (the growth bucket), and where it's being placed for protection (the income bucket). These sets can be broken down into various types of investment strategies based on where you are in your retirement. We'll discuss these, along with the income hierarchy pyramid, in chapter 5.

These three sets are intertwined, so it's difficult to talk about them in isolation. They have to be looked at together, and together they make up the "retirement smile," which corresponds to the costs associated with each retirement phase.

I've found that looking at retirement in terms of its progression (the Go-Go, Slow-Go, and No-Go Years) helps paint a better picture of what you can expect your golden years to look like as you combine the lifestyle and financial elements of retirement.

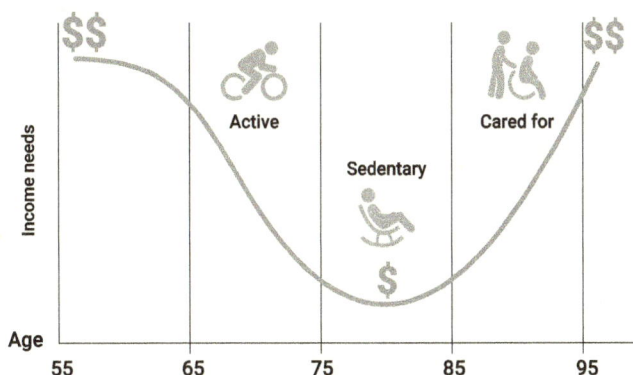

The Retirement "Smile"

Income needs change in retirement. For some, the more active early years of retirement requires more income to fund travel, hobbies, and home improvements, while the middle years become more routine and may require less. Later, depending on your health, you may need to budget for higher health care costs.

Source: Retire Wise, LLC

Most people go through three distinct phases of retirement: the Go-Go Years, the Slow-Go Years, and the No-Go Years.

———

CHAPTER 3

—

Retirement Risks

Retirement planning isn't just about saving enough money; it's also about preserving it and understanding and managing the potential risks that can affect your nest egg.

We tend to associate risk with investments, but even if you keep all your money tucked under the mattress, other forces, some more insidious than others, can erode your nest egg. For all the "mattress investors" out there, inflation and the resulting loss of purchasing power is an example of a risk you'll need to contend with, since mattress money can't grow.

Are these risks relevant in all phases of retirement? To an extent, yes.

Most people go through three distinct phases of retirement: the Go-Go Years, the Slow-Go Years, and the No-Go Years. These phases are exactly what they sound like. Each has different wants and needs, different ways of funding, and different ways to approach risk.

Retirement risks ebb and flow to some extent in each phase, and each risk has to be accounted for in the planning process. Even if you think, "I'll never be an aggressive investor," you never know what can happen health-wise, or with the economy, or with one of the biggest risks of all—outliving your money.

Retirement Risks

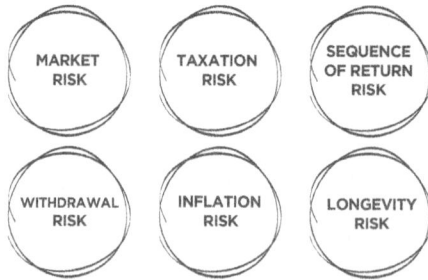

MARKET RISK

TAXATION RISK

SEQUENCE OF RETURN RISK

WITHDRAWAL RISK

INFLATION RISK

LONGEVITY RISK

Market Risk

When consumers speak of investment risk, they generally mean market risk—the possibility that an asset will lose value. Financial practitioners understand that there are several types of investment risk, including market risk, interest rate risk, credit risk, capital risk, timing risk, and inflation risk. To the average individual, investment risk means market risk. This perception is understandable when one considers the public's fascination with daily stock reports and mutual fund values, which seems to indicate that the only risk on anyone's mind is the value of their equity-based investment at any given moment.

As a general rule, common stock investments have been the best long-term hedge against inflation, but they're also the source of greater investment risk. Common stocks have more investment risk than preferred stocks, which are riskier than corporate bonds.

Investment risk is a serious concern that the wise investor will not dismiss lightly. Can you shield your nest egg by *not* investing? Not really. Retirees who tuck their retirement savings under the mattress or invest solely in low-yield assets that are shielded from investment risks expose themselves to the equally damaging effects of inflation. Put simply, retirees today face risk, in one form or another, whichever route they take. They must come to grips with the same two economic forces that keep younger investors constantly on edge: market risk and inflation risk. Retirement planning today demands equal attention to these opposing forces.

Investment risk has always figured prominently in the financial fears of retirees, particularly older retirees, who are prone to hold fixed-income investments that don't provide much hedge against inflation. Where the younger investor accepts this risk (perhaps with some reluctance) in exchange for potentially higher returns, some retirees dread it. While it may threaten the net worth of any investor, retirees view investment risk as a threat to the very heart of their retirement income.

Traditionally, the best defense against investment risk has been time. As long as the investment horizon reaches far enough in the future, the reasoning goes, a high level of investment risk is an acceptable trade-off for the above-average investment returns that such risk may yield. Time, however, is something a retiree does not have—at least not the time needed to justify an aggressive investment strategy.

As individuals approach retirement, understanding and managing market risk becomes a pivotal aspect of ensuring a secure financial future. Market risk, also known as systematic risk, refers to the potential for investment losses because of factors that affect the overall performance of financial markets. Let's look at the impact of market risk on retirement planning and the importance of strategies to mitigate this risk.

How Market Risk Can Affect Your Retirement

Market risk can have significant implications for retirees, primarily because it can erode the value of investment portfolios that are important for funding retirement. There are several types of market risks:

Portfolio Volatility

Market risk introduces volatility to an investment portfolio. For retirees who rely on their investments for a steady income, this volatility can lead to uncertainty in their financial stability.

Reduced Investment Returns

During periods of market downturns, the potential for reduced investment returns can compromise a retiree's ability to maintain their standard of living, as the income generated from investments may decrease.

Sequence of Returns Risk

The timing of market downturns can exacerbate market risk, particularly if negative returns occur early in retirement. This sequence of returns risk can have a huge lasting impact on the longevity of a retiree's savings. This risk is a big deal and deserves more conversation, so we have a whole section on this later in the book.

The Importance of Mitigating Market Risk

Mitigating market risk is essential for several reasons:

Preservation of Capital

Strategies to reduce market risk help preserve the capital you have worked hard to accumulate over your lifetime, ensuring that your savings will last throughout retirement.

Income Stability

By mitigating market risk, you can achieve greater stability in your investment income, which is crucial for covering living expenses and enjoying a comfortable retirement.

Confidence in Financial Planning

A well-structured plan to manage market risk provides you with confidence in your financial future, allowing you to focus on enjoying your retirement years without constant worry about market fluctuations.

Ways to Mitigate Market Risk

I strongly recommend avoiding a do-it-yourself approach when it comes to mitigating market risk, and I implore you to work with a seasoned financial planner. You can employ several strategies to mitigate market risk:

Diversification

A diversified investment portfolio can spread risk across various asset classes, reducing the impact of market volatility on the entire portfolio.

Asset Allocation

Adjusting the mix of assets and investment product types to include more conservative investments as you approach retirement can help protect against market downturns. Although to fight inflation and still have your portfolio grow, you need some money invested in the market. More on this later when we discuss inflation and bucket funding.

Annuities and Guaranteed Income Products

Investing in fixed and indexed individual retirement account (IRA) annuities (not variable) or other financial products that offer guaranteed income can provide a buffer against market risk, ensuring a steady income stream, regardless of market conditions.

Withdrawal Rate Adjustments

Modifying withdrawal rates during market downturns can prevent depleting your retirement savings too quickly.

Professional Financial Advice

Working with a financial advisor can help you develop and maintain a retirement plan that effectively manages market risk.

Market risk is an inevitable part of investing, but its impact on your financial health can be managed through careful and strategic planning. By understanding the implications of market risk and employing methods to mitigate it, you can help secure your financial future and enjoy the confidence that comes with a well-prepared retirement plan. Remember, retirement planning isn't only about growing your wealth; it's about preserving it to help ensure a confident and stable retirement.

Taxation Risk

Another risk that often goes overlooked is taxation risk—the uncertainty surrounding the impact of taxes on retirement income. Again, optimizing taxes is the principle of wanting to keep as much of your nest egg as you can for yourself and not giving more than your share to Uncle Sam. There are plenty of ethical and effective tax strategies that will keep more money in your pocket.

How Taxation Risk Can Affect Your Retirement

Taxation risk can significantly influence the amount of money retirees have available to spend. Here are some of the ways taxation risk can impact retirement planning:

Changing Tax Laws and Rates

Tax laws are subject to change. What may be a favorable tax environment today could shift in the future, potentially increasing your tax burden. This can reduce the after-tax value of retirement income, affecting your lifestyle and spending power. You may need to introduce strategies that can help protect your investments in case taxes go up in the future. I can tell you that at the time of this book, higher taxes are on the horizon.

Required Minimum Distributions

Retirees must begin taking required minimum distributions (RMDs) from certain tax-deferred accounts. The Secure Act 2.0, passed in December 2022, pushed the RMD age to 73 in 2023 and will further increase it to 75 beginning in 2033. These mandatory withdrawals can push many retirees into higher tax brackets, increasing their overall tax liability and reducing the amount of money they keep.

Social Security Taxation

Depending on other income sources, up to 85 percent of Social Security benefits may be taxable.[21] This can come as an unwelcome surprise to many retirees who haven't planned for these taxes impacting their expected retirement income.

If you have other provisional income in addition to your benefits, such as wages, self-employment, interest, dividends, and other taxable income that must be reported on your tax return, you will pay tax on your Social Security benefits based on IRS rules.[22]

- If you file a federal tax return as an individual and your income is between $25,000 and $34,000, you may have to pay income tax on up to 50 percent of your Social Security benefits.
- If your income is more than $34,000, up to 85 percent of your Social Security benefits may be taxable.

21   Angelica Leicht, "How Much of Your Social Security Income Is Taxable?," CBS News, March 6, 2025, https://www.cbsnews.com/news/how-much-of-your-social-security-income-is-taxable.

22   Leicht, "How Much of Your Social Security Income Is Taxable?" https://www.cbsnews.com/news/how-much-of-your-social-security-income-is-taxable/

- If you file a joint return, and you and your spouse have a combined income that is between $32,000 and $44,000, you may have to pay income tax on up to 50 percent of your Social Security benefits.
- If your joint income is more than $44,000, up to 85 percent of your Social Security benefits may be taxable.

This is what makes up the calculation for provisional income to determine if and how much taxes you would pay on your Social Security benefits:[23]

Your adjusted gross income
+ Nontaxable interest
+ 1/2 of your Social Security benefits

= Your "combined income"

Mitigating Taxation Risk
To manage taxation risk, consider the following strategies:

Diversifying Tax Treatments
Diversifying the tax treatment of retirement assets—such as a mix of taxable, tax-deferred, and tax-free accounts—allows for more flexibility in managing taxable income during

---

23   Kelley R. Taylor, "How to Calculate Taxes on Social Security Benefits in 2025," Kiplinger, April 28, 2025, https://www.kiplinger.com/retirement/social-security/604321/taxes-on-social-security-benefits

retirement. Incorporate each of these properly in your planning and distribution/drawdown plan in retirement.

Roth Conversions

Converting a traditional IRA to a Roth IRA can provide tax-free income in retirement. While this strategy incurs taxes at the time of conversion, it may be beneficial if you expect to be in a higher tax bracket in the future or if you feel tax rates will be higher. These conversions can also be stepped in stages so that you don't take the tax hit all at once. A financial advisor can model this to determine the best timing and strategy.

Tax-Efficient Withdrawal Strategies

Developing a tax-efficient withdrawal strategy can help minimize taxes over the course of retirement. This often involves drawing down taxable accounts first, followed by tax-deferred and then tax-free accounts. The whole drawdown plan needs to be coordinated across your various account types and align with your goals. The timing of this strategy and what funding buckets you withdraw from can have a big impact on the amount of taxes you pay. Your timing will also impact how long your money will last.

Working with a Financial Planner

A financial planner can help navigate the complexities of tax planning in retirement. They can provide personalized

THE PRIORITY OF RETIREMENT

advice and strategies to manage taxation risk based on individual circumstances.

Taxation risk is an important consideration in retirement planning that can have a substantial impact on your retirement financial well-being. By understanding potential tax implications and employing strategies to mitigate this risk, you can better preserve your hard-earned savings and enjoy a more stable retirement.

Inflation Risk

Another large impact on your retirement nest egg is inflation risk—the risk that the purchasing power of your income will decline because of rising prices. This is an especially critical concern for those retirees who are hesitant to invest their money. As life expectancies increase, the potential impact of inflation over the course of a retirement can be substantial. It can turn a retiree's initial financial comfort into eventual poverty. Let's consider what has happened over the last thirty years.

Inflation, as determined by the change in the Consumer Price Index for All Urban Consumers, has caused the cost of living to increase to such an extent that retirees in 1984 would need an income in 2018 equal to 242 percent of their 1984 income, just to make up for the income's lost purchasing power.

Let's do some comparisons between 1970 and 2020.

In January 1970 the Consumer Price Index (a way to measure inflation) was 37.8. In January 2020 it reached 258, a 683 percent increase in fifty years.[24]

At only 3 percent inflation, costs double every twenty-four years.

Although there is little question that many retirees can, and do, modify their lifestyles to accommodate generally rising prices, the simple replacement of today's prices onto tomorrow's possibly inflated economy is sobering. It is also a clarion call to retirement planning.

A financially comfortable person may eventually face serious financial hardship if the effects of inflation aren't considered and adequately addressed.

With today's retirement now being measured in multiple decades, inflation is a major issue that must be addressed in retirement planning. Now, along with wondering how to make your savings last through retirement, you must consider ways to make the value of that money last too. As a result, what was once seldom advised—adding some growth investments to your asset mix—is now an accepted part of more and more retirees' retirement planning.

Accepting a higher degree of market risk than historically recommended may be a practical way to keep up with inflation. When it comes to fighting inflation, the equity market may be the best game in town.

24   "Consumer Price Index Data from 1913 to 2024," US
      Inflation Calculator, accessed February 9, 2024, http://www.
      usinflationcalculator.com/inflation/consumer-price-index-and-annual-
      percent-changes-from-1913-to-2008/,

But how much risk is acceptable? That is, at what point does the right amount of aggressive investing become excessive and dangerous? How does one achieve the right proportions of investments between those that preserve assets and those that keep up with the rising cost of living? The answers are distinct for each person's situation. There are no one-size-fits-all answers.

How Inflation Risk Can Affect Your Retirement

Inflation risk can erode the value of your retirement savings over time. Here are some of the ways inflation risk can impact your retirement:

Decreased Purchasing Power

The most direct impact of inflation is the decrease in purchasing power. As the cost of goods and services rises, each dollar you have saved buys less. Over time this can significantly reduce your standard of living in retirement.

Fixed Income Vulnerability

Many retirees rely on fixed-income sources, such as pensions, Social Security, or annuities. While these are all key to retirement planning, they may not keep pace with inflation. This can lead to a gap between income and expenses, particularly as health care costs—which often rise faster than general inflation—become a larger portion of a retiree's budget.

Investment Strategy Challenges

Inflation can also affect investment returns. A portfolio that doesn't account for inflation may not generate enough growth to sustain a retiree's needs over the long term. This necessitates a careful balance between growth-oriented investments and more stable, income-producing assets.

Strategies to Mitigate Inflation Risk

To help protect against inflation risk, whether you're already retired or in the retirement planning stages, consider the following strategies:

Inflation-Adjusted Income Streams

Seek out income sources that can help protect against inflation, such as, such Treasury Inflation-Protected Securities, which adjust the principal value of the investment based on inflation.

Diversified Investment Portfolio

Maintain a diversified investment portfolio that includes assets with the potential to outpace inflation, such as stocks or real estate. While these investments come with higher risk, they can offer greater returns over the long term. These need to be factored in properly and in the right funding bucket, which we'll talk about later.

Flexible Withdrawal Strategy

Implement a flexible withdrawal strategy that can adjust for inflation. This may involve withdrawing a smaller percentage of your portfolio in the early years of retirement or adjusting withdrawals based on current inflation rates.

Health Care Planning

Plan for health care expenses, which often rise faster than inflation. Successful retirement plans often account for higher health care expenses. You can build this cost into your overall accumulation goals. You can also consider options like a Health Savings Account or purchasing long-term care insurance to help manage these costs.

Inflation risk is an unavoidable element of retirement planning, but with careful planning and strategic decision-making, its impact can be mitigated. By understanding the potential effects of inflation and implementing strategies to counteract them, retirees can better preserve their purchasing power and enjoy a more stable financial future.

Withdrawal Risk

Withdrawal risk has some related aspects to longevity risk and adds to the danger of outliving your retirement savings. The need to make regular withdrawals from your retirement funds to cover living expenses exacerbates this risk, as does the sequence of returns risk that we'll be discussing next. Without careful planning, there's a real possibility that you might deplete your resources too quickly, leaving you financially vulnerable in your later years.

How Withdrawal Risk Can Affect Your Retirement

Withdrawal risk can have several negative consequences for retirees:

Depletion of Retirement Funds

The most obvious impact of withdrawal risk is the potential depletion of retirement funds. If withdrawals are too large or the retirement portfolio underperforms, savings may run out sooner than expected.

Reduced Standard of Living

To avoid depleting your retirement funds, you may need to reduce your standard of living. This could mean cutting back on travel, leisure activities, or even basic necessities.

Dependency on Others

Retirees who outlive their savings may become financially dependent on government programs or on their family and friends, which can be a significant emotional and financial burden on all involved.

Strategies to Mitigate Withdrawal Risk

To manage withdrawal risk, retirees and financial planners can employ several strategies:

Establish a Safe Withdrawal Rate

One common approach is to determine a safe withdrawal rate, often suggested as around 4 percent of your total retirement nest egg annually, adjusted for inflation. This rate is designed to balance the need for income with the goal of preserving capital over a typical retirement span.

Utilize Annuities

Annuities can provide a guaranteed income stream for life, which can be an effective way to hedge against withdrawal risk. But it's important to use the appropriate type of annuity for an individual's situation. Utilizing a guaranteed income strategy has been recommended by such financial experts as Wade Pfau, PhD; Moshe A. Milevsky, PhD; Tom Hegna, economist and expert retirement specialist; Olivia S. Mitchell, PhD, economist; and Robert C. Merton, a recipient of the 1997 Alfred Nobel Memorial Prize in Economic Sciences.[25] We'll talk more about this strategy in a later chapter.

---

25   Pfau, "Protection as an Asset Class," Alliance for Lifetime Income, Retirement Income Institute, accessed May 30, 2025, https://www.protectedincome.org/research/protection-as-an-asset-class; Paul Feldman, "Don't Worry; Retire Happy—with Moshe Milevsky," InsuranceNewsNet, June 1, 2022, https://insurancenewsnet.com/innarticle/dont-worry-retire-happy-with-moshe-milevsky; Ben Mattlin, "Want 'Retirement Alpha'? Use Annuities, Says Insurance Veteran," Financial Advisor, June 16, 2023, https://www.fa-mag.com/news/use-annuities-for--retirement-alpha---says-author-and-insurance-veteran-tom-hegna-73586.html; "

Olivia S. Mitchell on Reducing Longevity Risk in Retirement," BusinessThink, University of New South Wales Sydney, April 14, 2024, https://www.businessthink.unsw.edu.au/articles/olivia-mitchell-retirement-planning-longevity-risk; Kathleen Coxwell, "Retirement Planning Should Focus on Income, Not Savings," Boldin, July 6, 2023, https://www.boldin.com/retirement/3-steps-to-a-retirement-income-plan-nobel-prize-winner-helps-you-figure-out-the-best-options.

By converting a portion of retirement savings into an annuity, you can ensure you have a steady income regardless of how long you live.

Build a Diverse Portfolio
A well-diversified investment portfolio can help manage market volatility and provide a mix of growth and income-producing assets. This can help sustain withdrawals over a longer period.

Plan for a Longer Retirement
I advise people to plan for a retirement that could last thirty years or more. By doing so, you can make more conservative estimates about withdrawal rates and investment returns. This ties into the longevity conversation, as life expectancies have risen and people are in retirement longer.

Review and Adjust Plans
Retirement plans should be reviewed and adjusted regularly to reflect changes in the market, inflation rates, and personal circumstances. This dynamic approach can help retirees stay on track and adjust your withdrawal strategy as needed.

Withdrawal risk is a significant concern in retirement planning, but it can be managed with careful and strategic planning. By understanding the potential impacts and employing methods to mitigate this risk, you can work toward a financially stable retirement. Remember, the goal isn't just to retire but to Retire Wise, helping to ensure a happy and secure post-career life.

Sequence of Returns Risk

Another huge risk in retirement (I put it in the top two risks) is the sequence of returns risk, which could undo years of careful planning. I'm shocked at how little this is talked about in the financial world. Knowing about the sequence of returns risk is important to a financially stable retirement.

If you plan to use money invested in the market as a source of retirement income, sequence of returns is the monster in the closet. Most people I talk to have never heard of sequence of returns risk, even if they're working with an investment advisor or broker. That's why you need a retirement advisor who also covers investments.

Many people don't realize that the last several years leading up to and especially the first few years of retirement can make or break your portfolio. Outside of longevity risk, the sequence of returns risk is one of the biggest risks retirees face.

That's why we're going to spend some time on this topic.

Many Americans wisely set aside money for the day they can stop working, kick back, and enjoy the twilight years of their lives. But be warned: The sequence of returns risk can trip up all your careful retirement planning.

The sequence of returns risk is defined as the order and timing of investment returns.[26] Here's how it works:

Once you retire, you no longer add money to your retirement account. Instead, you start taking regular withdrawals from your investment portfolio, and your nest egg begins to diminish. If your money is in the market, the returns you get on your investments—which can fluctuate wildly—become key to maintaining a reliable income stream. If stocks are at a low because of a big correction or crash, you're pulling money from much smaller account balances than in good market years. This could significantly reduce the longevity of your plan.

The timing of that correction or crash is critical. If it comes early in retirement, or just before you get there, it can seriously derail your plans. That's typically when you have the largest balances in your accounts and are more vulnerable to a major loss. If a correction or crash early in retirement causes a significant loss in value to your stocks, and you have to sell more shares to generate the income you need, this can affect whether your portfolio will bounce back or continue to be depleted faster than it should be. And even when the market recovers, you might not recover—you're out of runway.

If a correction or crash comes later in retirement when your nest egg is already smaller, it's less vulnerable to major

26   Kate Dore, "There's a 'Danger Zone' for Retirees When the Stock Market Dips. How to Shield Your Portfolio," CNBC, March 20, 2025, https://www.cnbc.com/2025/03/20/retirees-sequence-of-returns-risk.html.

losses. You may not have time to recover, but the hit you take will be less significant.

Your balance can be affected not only by how much your investments go up or down but also by when they go up or down.

Let's look at some facts and base information before we illustrate this significant risk.

Bear Markets

	Timeframe	Length in Days	% Change
1	June 1948 – June 1949	363	-20.57
2	August 1956 – October 1957	446	-21.63
3	December 1961 – June 1962	196	-27.97
4	February 1966 – October 1966	240	-22.18
5	November 1968 – May 1970	543	-36.06
6	January 1973 – October 1974	630	-48.20
7	November 1980 – August 1982	622	-27.11
8	August 1987 – December 1987	101	-33.51
9	March 2000 – September 2001	546	-36.77
10	January 2002 – October 2002	278	-33.75
11	October 2007 – November 2008	408	-51.93
12	January 2009 – March 2009	62	-27.62
13	February 2020 – March 2020	33	-33.92
14	January 2022 – October 2022	282	-25.40
	Average	344	-31.90%

Source: Retire Wise, LLC

- Since 1948, there have been fourteen bear market losses (defined as a 20+ percent loss), or about one every 5.7 years. If we go back further to 1929, there have been twenty-five bear markets (defined as a 20 percent loss), which brings the average to one about every 3.5 years.

- The average bear market lasts ten months and results in a 31.90 percent decrease.
- Few investors have the risk tolerance to emotionally accept a series of losses of 20+ percent losses.
- The timing of these downturns can adversely affect financial goals, such as college savings or retirement.

Few investors have the risk tolerance to accept a series of losses more than 20 percent. It's the *timing* of these losses that can be devastating if you don't have the luxury of riding out the current bear market. Considering a potential 30 percent loss, how do you get it back? What's the recovery time?

You must know your risk tolerance. This is more than your emotional state (some people are naturally more or less tolerant of risks). What's equally important here is your financial ability to ride out the stock market wave; in other words, where you've put your money, specifically in investment vehicles that are less vulnerable to market fluctuations.

If you start with	And you lose...	You are left with...	And you gain...	You are EVEN!
$100,000	10%	$90,000	11.1%	$100,000
$100,000	15%	$85,000	17.6%	$100,000
$100,000	20%	$80,000	25.0%	$100,000
$100,000	25%	$75,000	33.3%	$100,000
$100,000	30%	$70,000	42.9%	$100,000
$100,000	35%	$65,000	53.8%	$100,000
$100,000	40%	$60,000	66.7%	$100,000
$100,000	45%	$55,000	81.8%	$100,000
$100,000	50%	$50,000	100.0%	$100,000

Source: Retire Wise, LLC

Looking at the preceding chart, if we assume a 30 percent loss at a 3 percent rate of return, it would take 12 years to recover your base investment. If we double that return to 6 percent, it will still take 6 years to recover. If we get a really good 8 percent return, it will still take 4.6 years to get back to even. Remember, we see a bear market on average every 3.5 years. As a retiree, you may not have the luxury of decades of time to recoup your losses.

So does it still make sense to be in the market? For some, yes. Some have time to recoup and gamble on the market. For others, not so much. You should be aware of your unique situation.

Rate of Return versus Yield

Let's talk about rate of return (which I mentioned above) and yield.

Let's assume you have $500,000. If you invested in the market when it was shooting for the stars, and you were getting an absurd but welcome 50 percent rate of return, you made $250,000. Feels pretty good, right? Now you have $750,000 in your retirement fund.

After the big gain, what might come next? You got it: What goes up, must come down. Let's say the market tanks, and your investment goes down 50 percent in the second year. Here's the surprise. It's not what you're thinking—you won't lose 50 percent of the money you put in (that initial $500,000), but 50 percent of the current value. That brings us to a hefty $375,000 loss. But wait a minute! Plus 50 percent, minus 50 percent, wouldn't that be a zero rate of return? No. Remember, 50 percent of your initial $500,000 ($250,000) is not the same as 50 percent of your current portfolio value of $750,000 (half of which is $375,000).

Let's skip ahead to the third year where you get a positive 30 percent return (and you breathe a big sigh of relief). Thirty percent of $375,000 is $112,500. Add those together, and you have $487,500. But you started with $500,000. Wait a minute. What's going on? It's not magic; it's math. So you shouldn't be asking "What is my average rate of return?" You should always ask "What is my yield?

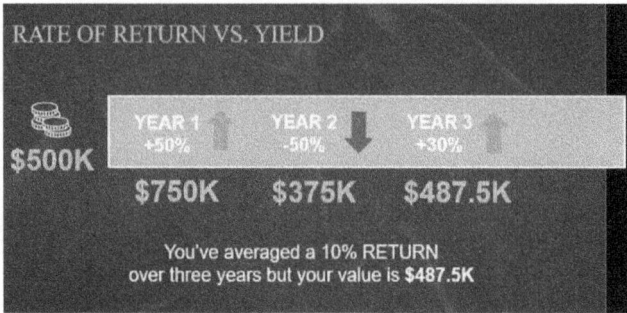

RATE OF RETURN VS. YIELD

$500K

	YEAR 1 ↑ +50%	YEAR 2 ↓ -50%	YEAR 3 ↑ +30%
	$750K	$375K	$487.5K

You've averaged a 10% RETURN
over three years but your value is **$487.5K**

This is a hypothetical example provided for illustrative purposes only; it does not represent a real life scenario and should not be construed as advice designed to meet the particular needs of an individual's situation

Case Study: The Potato Farmer's Yield

Carmen is a potato farmer. If Carmen buys potato seeds advertised at a six-potato rate of return, she would realistically expect to harvest six potatoes per plant. That is, given optimal conditions, each potato plant will have an average "rate of return" of six potatoes.

Just like what happens in the stock market, variables will influence each plant. Some variables can be controlled, some can't. Soil quality, water volume, insect infestation, the health of the individual plant, climate, and many other factors will affect the potato harvest. The yield (harvest) from each potato plant in the field can be vastly different. Some potato plants will yield six gigantic potatoes, while some will yield six scrawny fingerling potatoes. Some will yield one potato, while some will yield a dozen. Some plants will yield potatoes that grow too close to the surface and turn green (poisonous), meaning much of that harvest will have to be thrown out, while other plants will produce potatoes that grow deeper in the soil. Some plants will have a mix of small and large potatoes.

Even if Carmen gets six potatoes per plant, if potatoes are sold by the pound, and she's only able to sell baby potatoes, Carmen will have a smaller yield and a smaller harvest to take to market.

The average rate of return (six potatoes per plant) doesn't reflect Carmen's actual harvest (her actual yield).

What can Carmen do to help ensure a more consistent yield of six good-sized potatoes from each plant each season? She can strive to protect her plants from factors she can't control, such as weather. This could include planting potato varieties that are more suited to her particular climate and not those that are rock stars in a different climate. This could mean installing an irrigation system rather than relying on hand watering. This could mean planting potatoes a few inches farther apart. This could mean being prepared to quickly cover fragile plants from hail or insects.

Carmen will always have to contend with factors outside of her control, but by controlling what she can, she can protect her plants and give them a better chance to grow. By mitigating risk, Carmen is more likely to get a satisfactory yield from each plant at harvest time.

You can take a similar approach with your retirement portfolio to ensure optimized yields, even in the face of a significant market downturn. Yes, you'll have up years and down years due to factors outside of your control. But by controlling what you can, you will help to protect your portfolio, and your yield will be more consistent and predictable.

The problem is clear—and significant. What can you do about it? You can control the yield to the extent possible by working with a retirement planner. The route you take will be based on many diverse and unique factors.

The following example illustrates how important it is to diversify and to work with a financial planner who can counsel you on where to put your money so that it is less vulnerable to market fluctuations.

Case Study: Two Retirees, Different Results

Let's look at two retirees, Retiree A and Retiree B, who retired in different years, with different market conditions. Each retiree started with $1 million and made plans to withdraw $50,000 annually. Over the next thirty years, they experience the exact same average rate of return (6.3 percent). But based on the timing of their retirement and the current market conditions, let's see how the sequence of returns affected their portfolios.

Retiree A			Retiree B		
Year	Net Return	Year-end Value	Year	Net Return	Year-end Value
Beginning Balance		$1,000,000	Beginning Balance		$1,000,000
1	-17.50%	$775,000	1	9.90%	$1,049,000
2	-11.30%	$635,925	2	25.90%	$1,269,191
3	-4.60%	$553,627	3	17.60%	$1,439,524
4	9.60%	$551,973	4	6.60%	$1,479,896
5	-9.80%	$441,604	5	14.10%	$1,632,286
6	12.10%	$437,075	6	-19.70%	$1,252,752
7	13.10%	$434,629	7	1.80%	$1,170,509
8	18.40%	$453,107	8	16.20%	$1,298,638
9	6.00%	$416,955	9	8.60%	$1,346,983
10	-8.30%	$317,109	10	9.90%	$1,415,095
11	18.40%	$308,261	11	-0.30%	$1,343,654
12	7.20%	$261,244	12	25.60%	$1,618,418
13	-3.70%	$180,290	13	15.90%	$1,804,458
14	-1.00%	$105,061	14	23.60%	$2,156,884
15	13.00%	$43,089	15	16.90%	$2,445,768
16	16.90%	$0	16	13.00%	$2,685,819
17	23.60%	$0	17	-1%	$2,578,725
18	15.90%	$0	18	-3.70%	$2,400,670
19	25.60%	$0	19	7.20%	$2,488,397
20	-0.30%	$0	20	18.40%	$2,858,587
21	9.90%	$0	21	-8.30%	$2,531,018
22	8.60%	$0	22	6.00%	$2,589,865
23	16.20%	$0	23	18.40%	$2,970,595
24	-1.80%	$0	24	13.10%	$3,261,063
25	-19.70%	$0	25	12.10%	$3,554,012
26	14.10%	$0	26	-9.80%	$3,101,030
27	6.60%	$0	27	9.60%	$3,289,969
28	17.60%	$0	28	-4.60%	$3,027,566
29	25.90%	$0	29	-11.30%	$2,571,055
30	9.90%	$0	30	-17.50%	$2,003,292

Source: Retire Wise, LLC

Retiree A retired in 2000. Right away, he took a market hit up front since his retirement happened to coincide with a bear market, and his investments were in a more volatile category that was vulnerable to a market crash. The hit he took in those first three years of retirement nearly cut his savings in half. Despite several good years later on, he never recovered and eventually ran out of money halfway through retirement.

Retiree B retired in 2004 when the market was in better shape. She got off to a much better start with favorable bull market conditions. And though she had to endure some tough markets going forward, after three decades, she doubled her money to more than $2 million. You read that right. Even though she's withdrawing $50,000 per year, her investments have yielded significant gains because of the sequence of returns.

As you can see, the sequence of returns is crucial to retirement planning. You must have strategies in place to reduce this risk. In one scenario you're out of money halfway through retirement, and in the other you have over $2 million. In the second scenario (Retiree B), you could realize your retirement goals *and* leave a substantial legacy.

Don't take the sequence of returns threat lightly. You need to have a plan that prioritizes safeguarding the wealth you've accumulated.

You may be thinking "I can't control the market. Is there anything I can do?" Absolutely. You can't control the amount or order of your investment returns, but you can adjust your portfolio and your investing mindset to help minimize the sequence of returns risk. There are investment strategies that can help reduce this risk and even take it off the table.

Fortunately, there are ways to help protect and minimize any damage the sequence of returns risk can cause. You might find, for example, that it makes sense to reduce your exposure to volatility with a more conservative portfolio mix, invested in the proper investment vehicles for that stage of life. We can help you put together the proper investment mix. A thoughtful, prudent retirement income plan should provide protection strategies and flexibility when the markets are acting up.

Reducing your withdrawals after a crash or significant loss at the beginning of retirement is an option. You could also cash in other assets or reduce your living expenditures. But wouldn't you rather not have to do that? You're much more likely to enjoy a consistently comfortable retirement by having the proper comprehensive retirement plan designed and put in place.

This still means developing and sticking to a budget. Again, budgeting isn't meant to be an austerity measure that deprives you of the fun you should be having as a retiree.

There's nothing magic about the sequence of returns. The order in which the negative returns happen is the key. And while you can't control the market, you can take measures to preserve your portfolio.

As you can see from the case study, starting with $1 million didn't generate the same yields for the two retirees, even though their average rate of return was identical.

The protective measures we take will help ensure you have enough money to last throughout the entirety of your retirement.

Let's look at the different ways you can mitigate sequence risk.

In an enlightening 2017 article in *Forbes Magazine*, Dr. Wade Pfau described four ways to manage sequence risk: reduce volatility, spend conservatively, flexible spending, and buffer assets.[27] Two of the four are about reduced spending (such as the 4 percent rule), and the others are an attempt to reduce the volatility of the portfolio. The reduction in volatility means less time with a negative portfolio from which to potentially withdraw.

Buffer assets are a great and interesting concept. These assets are non-correlated with the stock market. More on this in a minute.

During downturns in the market, consider strategies and investments that may be less affected by the chaos:

- Build a lifetime spending floor with income annuities.
- Build a retirement income bond ladder.
- Use the rising equity glide path strategy (starting a portfolio conservatively and making it more aggressive over time).

As you approach retirement, you can begin to move some of your assets into lower-risk investments, such as bonds, that can help shield a portion of your money from market volatility. But you also give up potential for growth, so you might want to keep a certain amount of your port-

---

27   Wade Pfau, "4 Approaches To Managing Sequence of Returns Risk in Retirement," April 12, 2017, *Forbes Magazine*, https://www.forbes.com/sites/wadepfau/2017/04/12/4-approaches-to-managing-sequence-of-returns-risk-in-retirement/

folio in more aggressive investments. An alternative option to include in your plan, one that reduces risk and maintains some growth, is a deferred annuity.

Like many terms in retirement planning, "buffer asset" is a slang term, and Dr. Pfau derived the term from cash value life insurance's "volatility buffer." Buffer assets are those assets outside of your investment portfolio where returns aren't correlated with the stock market, so they can be used to prevent negative dollar cost averaging. That is, if the market is down, you don't have to sell low in order to maintain your income during retirement. Selling low and taking huge losses is a cardinal sin in investing. Instead, use (harvest) a buffer asset when the market is down.[28]

As an example of a buffer asset, Dr. Pfau cites cash value life insurance (permanent life insurance). You can "borrow" the cash value of a permanent life insurance product tax-free. The result of using this in a downturn to mitigate risk is impressive. The reverse home mortgage is another example. Both can be valuable tools/assets for retirement.

Variable spending strategies are important for retirement income planning. Logically and emotionally, this is what most retirees will do during down markets. Reducing spending after a portfolio decline is effective in mitigating the sequence of returns risk. It is also a natural behavior when the economy is in recession. The sequence of returns

---

28   Wade Pfau, "Adding Whole Life Insurance Cash Value as a Volatility Buffer in Retirement," Forbes, March 4, 2021, https://www.forbes.com/sites/wadepfau/2021/03/04/adding-whole-life-insurance-cash-value-as-a-volatility-buffer-in-retirement.

risk is partially mitigated here by reducing spending after a portfolio decline, thereby allowing more to remain in the portfolio to experience any subsequent market recovery. This alone won't prevent or mitigate the sequence of returns risk. You also need to implement some of the strategies listed above.

It's easy to see how these scenarios can play out in real life as you plunge into retirement. How long your money lasts could be affected by how well the market is doing when your retirement begins. You can, however, plan and put things in place to mitigate that risk.

A bull (positive) market those first few years of retirement would be good news. On the other hand, a bear (negative) market to start out could spell disaster. You need to do whatever you can to guard against a bear market. You don't want to work out those plans alone. Consult with a financial professional for careful planning that will sort out ways to reduce the chances that the sequence of returns risk will decimate your portfolio—and your retirement.

Longevity Risk

A risk associated primarily with the No-Go Years is longevity: the chance you might outlive your money. Longevity risk is the financial risk that retirees will outlive their assets, creating a gap between available resources and life expectancy. With advances in health care and living standards, people are living longer, making longevity risk a growing concern in retirement planning. As a result it's possible for people retiring at age sixty or sixty-five to look forward to a retirement that will be nearly as long as their working life.

Let's discuss the impacts of longevity risk and emphasize the importance of mitigating this risk to help ensure a secure and comfortable retirement.

It can be challenging to resist spending money during those heady early years of retirement. Many people choose to gamble that the market will remain strong or rebound in time for them to have enough in the later years. This approach often leads to poor outcomes, which can range from experiencing a lower quality of life to facing the severe issue of completely exhausting one's financial resources. You need to be clear on what you want your retirement to look like—including looking beyond the Go-Go Years to ensure there's enough left to fund the less active Slow-Go and health care–intensive No-Go Years.

Longevity risk arises from the uncertainty of life expectancy. While living a long life is a blessing, it also means that retirees need to plan for a longer period of financial self-sufficiency. We never know what the future will bring, but if you compare your health and expected longevity against what you expect to be doing throughout retirement, you'll have a better idea of how much to allocate to wants and wishes now versus in a decade or two.

How Longevity Risk Can Affect Your Retirement

The challenge is to ensure that retirement savings and income streams are sufficient to last throughout the retirement years, which could span decades.

Extended Retirement Period

A longer life translates into a longer retirement period, requiring more substantial savings to maintain the desired lifestyle without employment income. This means you need to recreate that paycheck in retirement for a longer period of time.

Increased Health Care Costs

Longer lifespans often come with increased health care needs, which can lead to higher medical expenses that must be factored into retirement planning. Estimates are that a couple who retires this year (2025) can expect to incur over $300,000 in health care costs in retirement, and the costs are expected to increase for future retirees.[29]

Another factor is long-term care cost. The latest statistics show that over 80% of Americans will need some form of long-term care in retirement.[30]

---

29   Bob Chitrathorn, "Planning for Health Care Costs in Retirement," Seniors Guide, May 8, 2025, https://www.seniorsguide.com/retirement-planning-elder-law-senior-finance/planning-for-health-care-costs-in-retirement/

30   Daniel de Visé, "If You Think You'll Never Need Long-Term Care in Retirement, You're Probably Wrong," USA Today, January 29, 2025, https://www.usatoday.com/story/money/2025/01/29/retirement-afford-long-term-care-insurance/77970635007.

Inflation Exposure

The longer retirees live, the more exposure they have to inflation, which can erode the purchasing power of their savings over time, as we discussed earlier.

Market Volatility

A longer retirement horizon means retirees may experience more market cycles, including downturns that can impact their investment portfolios. We discussed this at length in the section on sequence of returns risk.

Strategies to Mitigate Longevity Risk

Fortunately, there are a few ways to help prevent the possibility of outliving your money:

Annuities

Purchasing an annuity (fixed annuities can be a better option than variable annuities) can provide a guaranteed income stream for life, transferring the longevity risk to the insurance company.

Diversified Investment Portfolio

A well-diversified portfolio can help manage market volatility and provide growth potential to keep pace with inflation. This needs to be planned and balanced with the funding buckets we'll discuss later.

THE PRIORITY OF RETIREMENT

Delayed Social Security Benefits

Delaying Social Security benefits can result in higher monthly payments, which can be particularly beneficial for those who live longer than average. Social Security optimization is a process that will determine the right time and methods to file, as well as determine things like a break-even point if you delay your benefits. The Social Security office won't do this process for you; in fact, it's not allowed.

If you want to delay Social Security benefits to receive increased benefits, you can build what's called a Social Security bridge to fill the gap from your other retirement accounts. A retirement planner can assist with this plan.

Flexible Withdrawal Strategies

Adopting flexible withdrawal strategies, such as the 4 percent rule or dynamic spending rules, can help ensure that retirees don't outlive their assets. Be aware that the 4 percent rule is a default and was designed when the retirement landscape was very different and much more predictable. This rule is not right for all circumstances and needs to be evaluated on an individual basis.

Long-Term Care Insurance

Purchasing long-term care insurance can help cover the costs of extended health care needs without depleting retirement savings. But these policies can be expensive. If you're able, you can plan for the long-term care cost within your nest egg accumulation. There are also long-term care riders that can be placed on other investment vehicles that will pay for this eventuality.

Longevity risk is a significant factor in retirement planning that requires careful consideration and proactive management. By understanding the potential impacts and implementing strategies to mitigate this risk, you can better prepare for a financially stable and fulfilling retirement, regardless of how long it lasts. It's essential to work with a financial advisor who can tailor a retirement plan to your individual needs and help navigate the complexities of longevity risk.

Other Risks

Unfortunately, the risks we've covered so far aren't the only risks associated with retirement. Let's look at the rest.

No Margin/Low Margin Risk

A risk associated with any phase of retirement is not having enough margin. Another word for margin is "emergency fund," which can prevent your having to dip into retirement savings to cover unexpected expenses.

As we discussed in the previous chapter, you want to save a minimum of six months' worth of living expenses to help cover you in the case of an emergency without having to go into debt. Later in the book we'll discuss funding buckets and having enough money to live on for two to three years that will come from the right bucket and give you confidence in your investments. But before then, saving enough to cover six months is definitely possible, if you commit to it.

Your margin (emergency fund) should be considered a non-negotiable aspect of your budget.

Health Care Risk

A main risk associated with the No-Go Years is the ever-increasing cost of health care. Medicare barely scratches the surface of serious long-term health care challenges many seniors face.

Here's what Medicare.gov has to say about what's currently covered for those sixty-five and older.[31]

Medicare Part A (hospital insurance) "helps cover" inpatient hospital care, skilled nursing facility care, hospice care, and home health care.

Medicare Part B (medical insurance) "helps cover" eligible part-time or intermittent home health services as long as you are "homebound." Medicare defines homebound as needing assistance of a cane, wheelchair, walker, or crutches; special transportation; or help from another person to leave the home, and it's a major effort to do so. Homebound may also mean that it's impossible to leave your home because of a medical condition.

---

31   "What Medicare Covers," Medicare.gov, accessed February 9, 2024, https://www.medicare.gov/what-medicare-covers.

Covered home health services include the following:

- Medically necessary part-time or intermittent skilled nursing care
- Part-time or intermittent home health aide care, but only if you are also receiving skilled nursing care at that time
- Physical therapy, occupational therapy, and speech/language pathology services
- Medical social services
- Durable medical equipment
- Medical supplies for home use
- Certain drugs

Medicare also does not pay for the following:

- Twenty-four-hour in-home care
- Meal delivery to the home
- Housekeeping services, including cleaning and shopping, that aren't related to your care plan
- Personal assistance, such as help with dressing, bathing, or using the bathroom, if you do not require medical care

We don't need to go into the nitty-gritty here. Suffice it to say that these benefits are intended to be temporary, and they don't cover everything. Medicare doesn't cover long-term care.

This means that if your health situation requires long-term and full-time help, you'll need supplemental income to cover these costs. And as you'll see in Robert's case study in chapter 4, long-term care can be a significant expense.

Debt Risk

Coming into retirement with a lot of debt can mean giving away money to banks, not to mention the constant stress of having debt hanging over your head. We'll work together to prioritize debt elimination so that you can retire with little or no debt and put your hard-earned money to better use.

The next three chapters will discuss the typical phases of retirement and what they mean for you financially. You'll understand the importance of planning to ensure that each stage of retirement is comfortably funded.

CHAPTER 4

The Phases of Retirement

This chapter will outline the different phases of retirement (the Go-Go Years, the Slow-Go Years, and the No-Go Years) and how to fund them. Now that you know the risks to retirement, it's imperative to learn how different funding strategies come into play in each phase of retirement.

The Go-Go Years

For most people the first few years of retirement are like an endless vacation. They travel. They go back to school. They take up various hobbies. They remodel their homes.

They have plenty of energy, and they're excited to have the freedom of retirement.

Needs, Wants, and Wishes

Retirement is an expensive time. To avoid the tragic mistake of using up your entire retirement fund in the Go-Go Years, you must allocate funds to three categories: needs, wants, and wishes.

Needs

The needs category consists of your core expenses, including current and future living expenses (mortgage, utilities, insurance, taxes, debt, and other expenses that are non-negotiable). It's a good idea, if possible, to include planning for and funding future long-term health care costs from this category. The money may not be needed at first, so it can be shifted later if you're self-funding long-term care (more on that later). If you're purchasing long-term care insurance, the premiums can be included in the needs category.

Given that some of the money for your needs has to be liquid, we'll employ different strategies for continuing to grow your money during the go-go time as well as disbursing it wisely.

Unfortunately, for too many people, the needs category will take up most, and sometimes all, of their retirement funds. But that's okay. As long as your basic needs are met, you can participate in low- or no-cost activities and still find immense enjoyment in retirement. Such activities can include volunteering, which many retirees find rejuvenating and socially rewarding; gardening; walking, hiking, or other sports and fitness activities; learning a musical instrument or other creative hobby; or spending time with friends and family.

Wants

Once you've determined (and secured) your needs, we look at your closest desires. These are the things you want that would make retirement that much nicer: a little money for weekend getaways, a nicer streaming service, a few nights out every week, or whatever you defined for yourself earlier that would make your retirement more comfortable. Our goal is to put your wants within reach without endangering the needs category.

The wants category is achievable for many people. Obviously, the sooner you start saving for retirement, the better. With some wise choices, like eliminating debt, cutting back on expenses, and finding better investment vehicles, we can often set aside a healthy amount of money that will make retirement more fun.

Wishes

The wishes category includes your big dreams, the ones you think will probably never happen but would sure be nice. We're talking about a luxury trip to Europe, a sunroom addition to the house, a kitchen renovation, an RV trip to the National Parks, and other luxuries. For those with enough discretionary income, their wishes are achievable while still maintaining their needs and wants categories. For those without discretionary income, substitutes can be found that can be just as exciting and fulfilling.

Funding the Go-Go Years

Everybody has different plans and objectives for their retirement years, whether they want to see the world or take up interests they never had time for while they were raising a family and working. The transition, however, from earning income, saving, and investing to using that money in retirement may require a significant psychological change.

There are a lot of options for withdrawal plans besides the conventional 4 percent norm (which isn't for everyone). Withdrawal tactics vary widely, much like retirement plans, and there is no one-size-fits-all method. Retirement plans need to be personalized for each person.

The "bucket approach" is part of a drawdown plan that entails keeping three distinct buckets of money, each funding a different portion of your retirement years/stages, each with a specific purpose and investment strategy. The bucket approach has many proven advantages.

The bucket technique may offer psychological benefits as well, giving retirees a sense of security knowing that some assets and income streams are reserved for their projected future needs. This doesn't ensure that the investor will have sufficient funds for the retirement they have in mind, but it can help prevent disaster down the road.

During the Go-Go Years, the main emphasis is on the "liquidity bucket." The liquidity bucket is designed to cover immediate expenses and short-term needs, typically the first one to three years of retirement. This bucket is filled with highly liquid assets, such as cash, money market funds, and high-yield savings accounts to ensure that you have quick access to funds without having to sell investments at a potential loss during market downturns.

This isn't the only bucket that needs to be funded during the Go-Go Years. You also need to continue managing and funding the "income bucket" for the middle phase of retirement (the Slow-Go Years) as well as the "growth bucket," which will sustain you during the later retirement years (the No-Go Years). More on the bucket system later.

Common Blunders in the Go-Go Years

Social Security serves as one of the most important income sources for many retirees. According to the Social Security Administration (SSA), among people age 65 and older receiving Social Security benefits, these benefits represent about 31% of their income. Thirty-nine percent of men receive at least half of their income from Social Security; 12% of men receive at least 90% of their income from Social Security. For women the picture is similar: 44% receive at least half of their income from Social Security, and 15% receive at least 90% of their income from Social Security.[32]

---

32   "Fact Sheet: Social Security," Social Security Administration, 2025, https://www.ssa.gov/news/press/factsheets/basicfact-alt.pdf.

Yet retirees often don't put much effort into deciding when they'll file for those much-needed benefits.

When to begin taking Social Security benefits is not one size fits all. Some people take Social Security early, and it works for them: for example, those who are not well and don't expect to live a long time. For someone whose health and genetics suggest a much longer retirement, taking Social Security too early means lower income.

How and when you begin taking your benefits is a critical decision—even for higher earners. If you're married, your choices may someday affect your surviving spouse. Determining when and how to file is called Social Security optimization. Sometimes it makes sense to delay claiming benefits, and even if you still retire, you build that Social Security bridge to cover your expenses and needs to fill the gap until you file. This process also includes finding your break-even point if you delay filing. I can help guide you to the correct Social Security optimization and filing strategy.

The friendly folks at your local SSA office aren't authorized to make claims recommendations or help in this regard. And not all financial professionals are as experienced on this topic. I think you'll find it's worth your time to talk to us.

The Slow-Go Years

As we age, most of us slow down and no longer want to engage in the high-activity pursuits of our younger retirement. Your mind may say go, but the body begins to say no, and that's okay. For many, this is a phase of greater focus on family and community. People in this phase often enter what I call a volunteer career. Maybe they've done some volunteering in the past, but now being of service to others takes priority.

The slow-go lifestyle often means several years or even a decade of generally lower expenses.

Needs, Wants, and Wishes

I recommend periodic reassessment of your needs, wants, and wishes. Priorities can change. You may have done a lot of volunteer work during your Go-Go Years, and now you're ready to focus on a hobby you discovered through that volunteering. But don't feel like you're confined to a box. Let's sit down and clarify your revised needs, wants, and wishes so we can fund them appropriately.

Case Study: Jennifer

Jennifer took an early retirement at fifty, after a long career in the energy sector. Shortly before she retired, Jennifer's teenage daughter was participating in a high school–led community service project at an equestrian facility that offered therapeutic riding to people with physical and mental disabilities. Since her daughter wasn't driving yet, Jennifer drove her to the barn every weekend so she could catch, groom, and saddle horses; walk alongside the riders; and untack and release the horses. Instead of sitting on the fence for three hours watching her daughter, Jennifer thought, *Why not join the fun and do something meaningful?*

Jennifer had little experience with horses but quickly discovered she had a real affinity for them. Even better, she found herself able to relate to the riders, particularly those on the autism spectrum. Her calm, pleasant demeanor was exactly what timid riders needed to become comfortable on a horse.

Fast forward twenty-five years, and Jennifer is still a twice-weekly fixture at the facility. She continued to volunteer through two rounds of chemo for breast cancer and even returned to the barn four weeks after suffering a stroke, which, amusingly, made this self-proclaimed "extreme introvert" much more sociable and, in her own words, "downright chatty." She told me, "I said probably fifty words in seventy years, but after the stroke, you can't shut me up."

Jennifer's situation is a classic retiree story. "If I didn't start volunteering here," she said, "I would probably be sitting in my living room wasting my life on daytime TV. But here I am, feeling more alive than ever. I am outside in this spectacular setting in the California hills. I am making a difference for these riders whose lives are so much more challenging than mine. I forget my problems when I'm there. I stop being that breast cancer survivor who had a stroke. I become that woman who puts a smile on people's faces because they had a great ride alongside me. Everybody has a story. I've heard so many stories from people I probably wouldn't have ever met had it not been for the barn."

Partly to get out of the house and partly because of a desire to give back, retirees often find a new passion and a new purpose as volunteers. Volunteering doesn't cost a thing, which can help ease the financial stress of wanting to live a fulfilling life but not having the means to contribute financially to charitable causes.

Funding the Slow-Go Years

The Slow-Go Years are often accompanied by a desire to pare down to the things that really count. In many cases, these things have no cost. Many retirees will also want to downsize, which can free up a significant amount of money that was previously held as equity.

The Slow-Go Years are ideally funded from the income bucket. The income bucket is designed to generate steady income for this mid-term phase of retirement, usually covering years anywhere from four to ten. The funding buckets are staggered but related to each other, and they flow from one to the other.

The income bucket may include fixed-income investments like bonds, annuities, or dividend-paying stocks that provide a reliable stream of income while still offering some potential for growth to keep pace with inflation. It is key to include investment vehicles that provide you guaranteed income (partial paycheck replacement) that is less affected by market fluctuations.

There's a certain relief in receiving guaranteed income payments that cover basic costs and include some "fun money." Guaranteed income comes in the form of Social Security, a company pension if that's an option, or fixed and indexed annuities that you purchased or invested in. The annuities effectively provide a personal pension of your own.

It's important to start saving for retirement as soon as possible and also eliminate debt that can significantly erode your nest egg. Clients often find that they can "live on air" (have barely any expenses outside of their housing and daily living expenses) when they have no credit card debt, no car payments, and no mortgage. Imagine the freedom a debt-free retirement can bring.

Common Blunders in the Slow-Go Years

Some people want to leave money to their kids, but there's a right way and a wrong way to do this. Now is the time to consider your legacy.

Individual retirement accounts are, by their very nature, meant to be depleted over the account owner's lifetime. Indeed, the IRS encourages it. Even if you don't want or need to withdraw the money during your retirement, you must take RMDs every year. Your first RMD must be taken by April 1 of the year after you turn seventy-three. Subsequent RMDs must be taken by December 31 of each year. If you don't take your RMD, you'll have to pay a penalty according to IRS guidelines.[33] But what if you don't empty

---

33   "IRS Reminds Retirees: April 1 Final Day to Begin Required Withdrawals from IRAs and 401(k)s," IRS, updated May 29, 2025, https://www.irs.gov/newsroom/irs-reminds-retirees-april-1-final-day-to-begin-required-withdrawals-from-iras-and-401ks.

the account and, instead, leave the money behind for your children?

Recent changes in the tax laws will give your kids only ten years to empty the account, and they'll pay taxes based on their tax bracket, not yours, at the time they make those withdrawals. If they happen to be in their highest-earning years (which is often the case), a large chunk of the money your children would have enjoyed could end up going to the IRS.

If you've socked away the bulk of your savings in a tax-deferred account (a 401(k), 403(b), traditional IRA, etc.), you're not stuck. During your lifetime, there are ways you can change taxable dollars into nontaxable dollars, such as a Roth IRA conversion. Past 401(k)s and 403(b)s that are getting hit by high fees and risk can be rolled over into better investment vehicles.

Life insurance is a way to leave a legacy to your children, one that costs pennies on the dollar compared to giving away your nest egg. Why not have the boat, the country club membership, and the dream vacations, and enjoy the retirement you worked hard for all those years? If you hold back and don't enjoy your nest egg, your kids will buy the boat, the membership, and the vacations. I'm not saying don't leave a legacy to your children, but you can have your happy retirement *and* leave something for your kids, if you choose to.

Pursuing your retirement dreams is challenging enough without making these common blunders. As you listen to other tips and tales, keep in mind that real knowledge is power. Don't hesitate to ask for professional guidance when designing your retirement income and retirement tax plans.

The No-Go Years

For most retirees, health challenges mean greater expenses toward the end of their lives. Failure to plan for poor health can be disastrous. Whether or not you will ever have the need for an assisted living facility, a nursing home, or a long-term home-care service, don't take the chance you won't need it. Plan for it. It's a bonus if you never have to use it, but it must be considered.

Don't take good health for granted. Plan for the worst-case scenario, and pray it never materializes.

Case Study: Robert

Robert was a successful small business owner who refused to stop working just because of his age. At seventy-four he was still going strong. He went to the office every day, and he continued to pursue his lifelong passion for competing in triathlons. He looked and acted decades younger. To say Robert was an inspiration to everyone is an understatement.

One day while playing tennis with friends, Robert suffered a stroke. He blacked out and hit his head on the concrete surface. The stroke left Robert paralyzed on the left side of his body, unable to speak, with a host of emotional and personality changes.

Robert's stroke changed his life. He was single and didn't have any family who could help him, so he chose to go into a nursing facility. He had basic Medicare coverage (having refused more comprehensive insurance because he had taken the attitude of "I won't need it; I'm healthy"). He also hadn't seen the need for long-term care insurance or planning for long-term care with his investments.

Robert was used to nice things. At first he insisted on having a live-in home health aide, but after going through several who didn't work out, he moved into the nursing home. But not just any facility would do. Robert didn't want to live somewhere that looked like, in his words, "an insane asylum." Because of the astronomical cost of a good nursing facility, Robert was forced to sell his home. He also sold his business when it became apparent he wouldn't be able to return to work. While these assets were significant, they, along with his $500,000 nest egg, were barely enough to cover 24/7 care at the nursing facility as well as costs not covered by insurance, until he passed away at age ninety-five.

What would have happened if Robert didn't own a business he was able to sell for nearly a million dollars? What would have happened if he didn't own a home and had barely 40 percent equity? What would have happened if he didn't have any savings? All told, Robert's nursing home bills amounted to about $9,000 a month. That's $108,000 a year. The final nursing home tab was $2.27 million from the time he entered the facility after becoming paralyzed from a stroke to when he passed away twenty-one years later. That doesn't even count various other expenses that insurance didn't cover.

Medicare generally doesn't cover the cost of nursing homes. Robert didn't qualify for Medicaid, which put him in the position of having to pay for it out of pocket.

Can you wrap your head around $2.27 million? For most Americans with little or no retirement savings, this would be financially devastating. It's no wonder that 550,000 people file for bankruptcy annually because of medical debt.[34] While you may not have the opportunity to amass several million dollars "just in case," being as prepared as possible is not negotiable in this day and age. You *must* plan for this contingency as part of your needs category funding.

Research long-term care insurance, as there are several options in these policies. You need to carefully time these policies though so you don't pay premiums too early or face unaffordable premiums if you wait too long. You can also self-fund your long-term care from your investments, if you're able to, and make it part of your overall planning. There are also some investment vehicles that have riders you can add, which will help pay for long-term care.

---

34   John August, "Healthcare Insights: How Medical Debt Is Crushing 100 Million Americans," Scheinman Institute blog, School of Industrial and Labor Relations, Cornell University, October 21, 2024, https://www. ilr.cornell.edu/scheinman-institute/blog/john-august-healthcare/ healthcare-insights-how-medical-debt-crushing-100-million-americans

Funding the No-Go Years

The third bucket, the growth bucket, is focused on long-term growth and is meant to fight inflation and any market fluctuations to sustain you in the later stages of retirement, beyond ten years. The growth bucket is typically invested in a diversified portfolio of stocks, mutual funds, and other growth-oriented assets. These investments are often higher risk/higher yield, but everyone has a different risk tolerance and may not feel comfortable riding out the roller coaster of market fluctuations.

The goal is to achieve higher returns over the long run, which are essential for maintaining purchasing power, fighting inflation, and covering expenses later in retirement when other buckets may be depleted. More later on how the buckets work with each other and how they flow and replenish each other.

Common Blunders of the No-Go Years

Outliving your money becomes a real danger and is a primary risk in retirement, as we discussed earlier, especially if you haven't set up a plan for long-term health care and if you haven't paid enough attention in previous years to adding to your growth bucket.

A person who turns sixty-five today has about a 40% chance of needing 'high intensity' long-term care for at least a year.[35] Most married couples think they will provide this

---

35   de Visé, "If You Think You'll Never Need Long-Term Care." https://www.usatoday.com/story/money/2025/01/29/retirement-afford-long-term-care-insurance/77970635007/

care for each other, but that isn't always possible, and it can devastate the health of a caregiver who isn't physically or emotionally equipped to deal with a loved one's needs. Naturally, this doesn't apply to people who are single or don't have family who can shoulder the caregiving burden.

The good news is that there are several solutions, including fixed indexed annuities providing guaranteed income, long-term care insurance and life insurance plans that offer cash values, and accelerated medical and death benefits. The annuities today have more flexibility and options and can be a good choice for your plan. Many retirees think they don't need life insurance once they reach a certain age, but there are benefits to be had. Again, each plan and person is different; it's not one size fits all. Together, we can choose the right products for your needs.

CHAPTER 5

The Drawdown Strategies

I t's been said that the journey off the mountain is much more perilous than the journey up. As you're going up, you're focused on the summit, and you put all your energy into standing up there. When you're working, your money is accumulating; at the point of retirement, you're standing at the top of the mountain with this amazing view. But the journey doesn't stop there. You have to make it safely back down to basecamp.

How and when you withdraw your money is the next step in the retirement planning process. This chapter will discuss the bucket strategy and the income hierarchy pyramid, which offer two related ways of looking at how to wisely spend your nest egg (and still have fun).

The Income Hierarchy Pyramid

The income categories in retirement are another way of looking at how each phase of retirement will be funded. Buckets and pyramids may seem unsophisticated, but they present excellent visuals that help people who aren't money wizards understand how retirement actually gets funded.

The income hierarchy pyramid is a handy tool that helps you define a sustainable retirement budget. You won't be remotely satisfied or happy if you can't pay your bills. It's not fun to lay awake at night wondering how you're going to pay the electric bill. That kind of stress can manifest later as chronic disease.

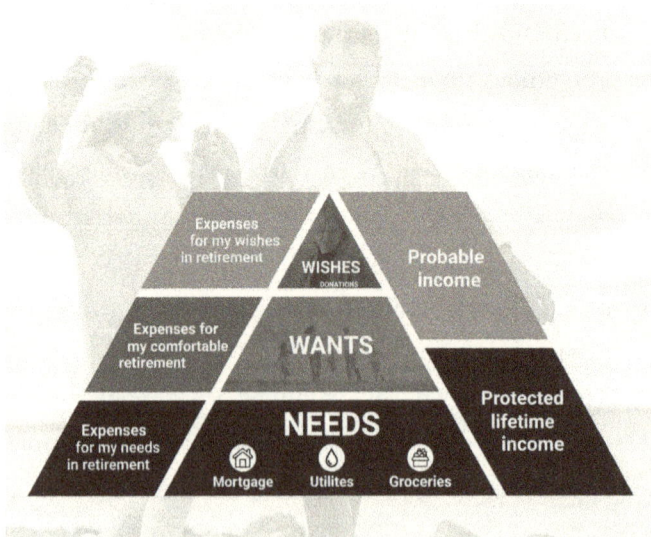

Source: The Alliance for Lifetime Income. Used by permission under License #5325021.

The bottom of the income hierarchy pyramid is the financial foundation: your needs category. Figuring out a sustainable budget for retirement isn't any different than coming up with a budget while you're working. You can plan ahead by modifying your current budget to account for non-working years—removing things you won't have anymore, like the costs of a commute, a work wardrobe, or maybe a mortgage payment.

You'll also need to consider that your tax bracket will be different. I like to be extremely specific with budgeting so that there aren't any surprises, like forgetting to pay the property tax because it was normally rolled into your mortgage payment.

On average most retirees find that they need about 75–80 percent of their working income during retirement. If you go on expensive vacations, you'll need more. But if your home is paid off and you have no other debt, you could need just 40–45 percent of your working income. It's different for each person or couple. I've seen it be anywhere from 40 percent to 90 percent.

It's important that we don't guess about how much money you'll need during retirement. Being armed with knowledge is a critical step to a financially stable retirement.

One side of the bottom part of the pyramid outlines your core needs, including every cost associated with everyday living: housing, utilities, transportation, clothing, personal care, groceries, pet care, insurance. I also include long-term health care in the needs bucket even though you may never need it, and if you do, it's probably off in the future. You need to start saving or investing for long-term care as soon as possible to take care of this eventuality.

I always say you don't have a complete retirement plan unless you have a long-term care health plan. Long-term health care falls in the top part of the needs section because it's a future cost for most people. If I had to prioritize things in that needs bucket, long-term care takes less precedence than your current mortgage, utilities, and basic everyday living needs, but it still has to be in there.

Some people can afford to put money toward long-term care or long-term care insurance, and some can't. But there are options. Whether or not you can or want to buy long-term care insurance, we always discuss a long-term care strategy. You can also put a portion of your investment portfolio aside for long-term care or use investment vehicles that have riders on them to fund long-term care.

Let's talk about how your needs are going to be funded.

The right side of the pyramid shows something called "protected lifetime income." This is guaranteed retirement income and that's what should fund your core needs. Guaranteed retirement income includes Social Security, pensions, and annuities. These are the main three, but there may be a few other sources we can tap into.

The next level up shows expenses that ensure a more comfortable retirement. These are your closest desires, your wants, the things you would love to do that would make your retirement a little more comfortable. The wants relate to the little things, like a bigger entertainment budget or money for a once-monthly weekend getaway. Depending on the scope of your wants, you might be able to fund these little luxuries from the same source as your needs (from your protected lifetime income).

We want to ratchet up the retirement happy factor a little bit where we can, with niceties that are meaningful to you and with the activities that fall under your purpose. If travel is important to you, it's a want but an essential one. Your protected lifetime income should still be able to at least partially fund many of your wants. It's so important to be discerning here. We want to avoid dipping into funds that you'll need as time passes.

At the bottom of that initial wants section are the comfort things. At the top are the purpose-driven things. Ideally, we try to fund at least 50 percent of your wants with protected lifetime income. Some people may be able to fully fund their needs and wants from their protected lifetime income. For the rest of us, aiming for at least 50 percent is the goal.

At the top are your wishes. Those are the dreams, the extra fun things like the trip to Europe or even finally buying that dream house. If you had the money, what are some of those things you dream about? What have you always wanted to do? Those things can put you over the top in the happiness factor. I encourage everyone to think big. Why not? Go for it, especially if you're someone who started planning early. The earlier you plan, the more chances you have to get to the top of the pyramid.

Even if you've started saving for retirement later in life, you can still use this pyramid as a guideline. The pyramid will help you get through the foundation and secure your needs, and hopefully address some or all of the wants. As a bonus, you may even get to enjoy some of your big wishes. Wherever you are, you can still apply these principles. Just know that when you start and how much you're able to put away will determine how far you can take your wishes.

None of the wishes are funded from protected lifetime income. "Probable income" (from investments that may fluctuate over time, the more risky investments) funds your wishes. Imagine how devastating it would be to fund your needs from probable income. You would never sleep soundly at night. Needs are typically funded from the protected lifetime income bucket.

I typically do a risk tolerance assessment with my clients. Some people are risk-averse and would rather be assured of smaller incremental gains than risk losing a large chunk of their nest egg. Others, especially those with a generous margin, may be adventurous investors with more leeway in how they invest money to fund today's as well as tomorrow's wishes.

Your protected lifetime income may not be enough to pay off debt in addition to your daily living expenses, which can become problematic. That's why I urge people to get rid of debt before they retire. Whatever it takes—perhaps living frugally for a couple of years—will be worth it in the long run because you won't need to be pulling from your predicted income to pay the banks. I talk about giving as a cornerstone of being happy in retirement, but we certainly don't have to be generously giving to the banks. We can give to better causes than the banks.

Another way to look at debt is through the happy factor meter. We all have one ranging from "empty" to "full." Stressed, broke, and unhappy lands the needle on empty. Happy, financially secure, and fulfilled lands the needle on full. What can move the needle in the right direction? Debt certainly isn't landing you on full.

Where things can get tricky is that each phase of retirement, each bucket, and each step of the pyramid has to be funded and budgeted differently. This is where working with a financial planner can be the difference between growing your portfolio while enjoying a retirement income and eroding your nest egg with no clear plan for the future.

The Bucket Strategy

The previous chapters touched on which of your funding buckets are intended to fund each phase of retirement. Now let's go deeper into the bucket strategy so you can understand how wise investing and wise distribution can help the income bucket and the growth bucket overflow and trickle down into the liquidity bucket, which allows you to create the most enjoyable retirement scenario during the Go-Go Years and even into the Slow-Go Years.

The bucket plan is a strategic and intuitive way to organize your retirement savings. By addressing the various risks associated with retirement and providing a clear framework for asset allocation, the bucket plan can help retirees navigate their golden years with greater confidence.

Benefits of the Bucket Plan

When you're working, you're in the accumulation phase. You and your money are going up, up, up to the summit of a mountain. Your portfolio is growing, and because you have time, you may be able to take more investment risks. Your margin goes up.

When you reach the summit, which is the point of retirement, you've reached what I consider the biggest danger zone. Here, you must look to the future. You can't take as many risks. You need to start preserving your primary source of income; in other words, you have to do what it takes to help ensure that you have enough protected lifetime income throughout retirement. This includes mitigating retirement risks like the sequence of returns risk and longevity risk, as well as performing Social Security optimization and so forth.

Once you're on that downward journey, you're not accumulating any more money. Even if your investment portfolio continues to grow, you're not taking a traditional work paycheck. On the way down the mountain, you don't want to take risks. You want to basically recreate your paycheck. Whatever is left over, you can invest in a mixed portfolio that looks toward the immediate future, near future, and distant future with different strategies.

The disbursement phase of retirement—the journey back down the mountain—can be incredibly treacherous if you don't plan for it. Why? People put a lot of energy and thought into accumulating wealth, but they don't think much about how to use that wealth to recreate their paycheck *sustainably* and fill those buckets *regularly*. Which funds do you draw down first and on what schedule? When should you start collecting Social Security? How can you minimize taxes? We create a drawdown plan that's as detailed as the accumulation plan.

The bucket plan offers several advantages for retirees:

- **Risk management:** Retirees can reduce the impact of market volatility on their immediate income needs when they allocate assets according to when they will be needed.
- **Inflation protection strategies:** The growth bucket allows for continued investment in assets with the potential to outpace inflation, preserving the purchasing power of your savings.
- **Flexibility:** The plan can be adjusted based on changing needs, market conditions, and personal circumstances.
- **Clarity and confidence:** A structured plan can provide confidence, knowing that you have a strategy to fund each phase of retirement.

Work with a financial planner to implement and optimize the bucket plan according to your budget and your retirement vision. Together, you will carry out the following tasks:

- Assess your financial situation and retirement goals.
- Determine the appropriate amount of funds to allocate to each bucket, and divide your retirement assets into separate buckets based on periods of time (or the anticipated phases of retirement).
- Select investments that align with the objectives of each bucket.
- Monitor and rebalance your buckets as needed to help ensure they remain aligned with your retirement timeline and risk tolerance.

Depending on your priorities and preferences, you may wish to add additional segmentation, or at least keep a greater number of assets in the third bucket, especially if you plan for a long retirement. As a proportion of the US population, the number of centenarians has been steadily increasing,[36] suggesting that more people are likely to be enjoying thirty or more years of retirement.

Anyone who is gradually depleting their nest egg and might eventually need to sell their investments to cover

---

36   Karen Mansfield, "Number of Centenarians Expected to Quadruple over Next 30 Years," Observer-Reporter, March 20, 2025, https://www.observer-reporter.com/news/local_news/2025/mar/20/number-of-centenarians-expected-to-quadruple-over-next-30-years/#:~:text=Mar%2020%2C%202025%20By%20Karen%20Mansfield%203%20min%20read&text=The%20number%20of%20centenarians%20in,based%20on%20Census%20Bureau%20figures.

living expenses can benefit from the bucket strategy. With the bucket approach, you can group the assets that you may want to sell off during each retirement phase while maintaining the most appropriate asset allocation strategy for each bucket.

Funding Strategies for Each Bucket

How do you fill your buckets?

First, calculate your annual living expenditures during your working years. Use that as the foundation for your retirement income. Don't forget these critical steps:

- Deduct work-related costs such as commuting, a work wardrobe, etc.
- Add extra money for an emergency fund in case you have unforeseen expenses when creating the first bucket.
- Forecast your spending for the next few years, accounting for inflation and any one-time expenses like a child's wedding or an expensive vacation.

Then, look at a second category of retirement expenses— your wants, or money to cover costs that aren't mandatory but that you would really like to afford. Add this to your basic income requirement (but itemize it separately in case you need to make compromises based on your retirement savings and budget).

Next, allocate the appropriate strategies to the various buckets.

With the bucket approach, you divide your retirement assets into separate buckets of assets based on periods of time. Those time horizons can be flexible, as can be the number of buckets, but three is a common choice. Here are a couple of examples.

Retirement bucket strategy

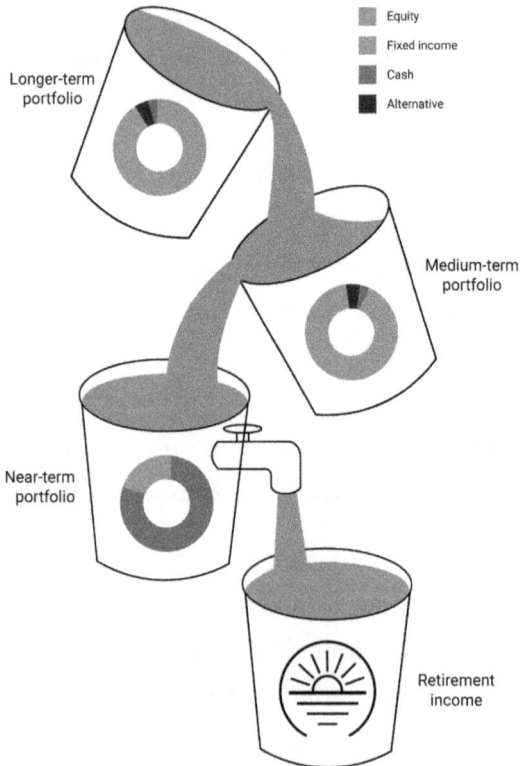

Source: Retire Wise, LLC

The Liquidity Bucket

The liquidity bucket is characterized by liquidity and low risk. A combination of cash, money market funds, high-yield savings accounts, and a CD ladder could be in this first bucket. Remember, this should also include an emergency fund of at least six months of living expenses.

The Income Bucket

The income bucket may consist of investments that are typically seen as lower risk. This second bucket is intended to generate steady income for the mid-term phase of retirement, usually covering years four to ten. This bucket may include fixed-income investments like bonds, annuities, or dividend-paying stocks that provide a reliable stream of income while still offering some potential for growth to keep pace with inflation. There is also the option of Treasury Inflated-Protected Securities. These are flexible but still fairly safe investment options for a percentage of your portfolio. With all these options, you'll enjoy periodic payouts of inflation-protected income to fund your wants and potentially some of your needs.

Early in retirement you're not dipping into this bucket yet, but you need to be careful not to jeopardize this bucket with more aggressive investments that carry higher yields but also higher risk.

The Growth Bucket

The growth bucket has the greatest time horizon, may be devoted to growth, and often contains higher-risk/higher-yield investment strategies that will help fight inflation and fund future expenses including, wherever possible, your wishes.

This third bucket is designed to weather market fluctuations. You shouldn't have to worry about being forced to sell long-term investments from the growth bucket in the event of a market downturn if you have other buckets to pay your immediate costs, since these assets typically won't be needed for over a decade.

Invest funds that are intended for discretionary expenses according to your values and risk tolerance. This third bucket is also focused on long-term growth and is meant to sustain you in the later stages of retirement, beyond ten years. This bucket is typically invested in a diversified portfolio of stocks, mutual funds, and other growth-oriented assets. The goal is to achieve higher returns over the long run, which are essential for maintaining purchasing power and covering expenses later in retirement when other buckets may be depleted.

Remember that each bucket is funding three different timelines and three different financial elements: needs, wants, and wishes.

The rationale behind allocating specific asset classes to each bucket is to enable you to allocate more risky assets to your long-term bucket, enabling you to weather market fluctuations. In essence, we're talking about creating income for your entire retirement, which is why it's essential to break up each "lump sum" (the value of each asset) into how much it can contribute to your retirement income in a given year.

Think about these buckets stacked one on top of another in the same order as the pyramid: the liquidity bucket at the bottom, the income bucket in the middle, and the growth bucket at the top. You must periodically review and rebalance the funds in the buckets to replenish as they flow from the top down to fund all your phases of retirement.

ONE POSSIBLE CHOICE	HERE'S ANOTHER CHOICE
BUCKET 1: 0-5 YEARS	BUCKET 1: 1-3 YEARS
BUCKET 2: 6-10 YEARS	BUCKET 2: 4-7 YEARS
BUCKET 3: 11+ YEARS	BUCKET 3: 8+ YEARS

Source: Retire Wise, LLC

If you fill the needs category with protected lifetime income and the rest from probable income, chances are good that the wishes and wants categories will overflow and help fund the buckets below (because you're using more aggressive investment strategies with higher yields). You use different investment and budgeting strategies to ensure that a) all needs categories are always full, b) you're not pulling too much from the buckets you'll use later, to enjoy today, and c) different investment strategies will support larger future gains that can help replenish any shortfalls from the more current buckets.

As you develop your bucket plan, be sure to factor in the sequence of returns risk (when and how you take withdrawals as well as the sequence and timing of unsatisfactory investment results).

If there is a significant decline in your portfolio during the initial years of your retirement, there is a risk. You will need to sell a larger percentage of your investments in order to raise a fixed amount of cash if you take out loans against your portfolio to cover living expenses while it is depreciating. This not only depletes your retirement savings earlier than anticipated but also leaves you with less assets to grow your money with in the event that the markets rebound in the future.

Here's where the bucket method comes in handy. You can pay your bills without taking money out of your stocks and other long-term growth investments by using your first bucket of short-term, low-risk liquid holdings, which should consist of cash and cash equivalents. Putting a year's worth of expenses in cash investments in that first bucket, and another two to three years' worth of costs in premium cash equivalents is one way to go about it. With that kind of cushioning helping to protect you from market swings in your growth bucket, you should be able to weather market losses while you wait for the market (stocks/equities) to perhaps rise again in the future.

By addressing the various risks associated with retirement and providing a clear framework for asset allocation, the bucket plan can help retirees navigate their golden years with greater confidence. As with any financial strategy, it's important to consult with a financial professional to tailor the plan to your unique situation and ensure that your retirement goals are met.

Your bucket plan will be unique to you and your retirement goals and needs. Some people have their money in IRAs, Roth IRAs, pensions, annuities, cash value life insurance policies, stocks, various other investment vehicles, and even cash under the mattress (though not recommended). Some are tax-deferred, some are tax-free, and some are taxed regularly.

I can't stress enough that your goal should be to optimize various guaranteed income vehicles for part of your retirement nest egg. This is something we would consider a key happy factor. There's pure math and science behind these vehicles, and they've been recommended by PhDs, Nobel Prize winners in economics, and renowned economists and retirement experts, including the founder of the 401(k) (which is not a form of guaranteed income).

What others are saying about guaranteed income vehicles:

- Center for Retirement Research at Boston College in 2021: "Guaranteed lifetime income products are a cornerstone of retirement planning."[37]
- BlackRock, a multinational investment company: "Adding guaranteed lifetime income combined with a more aggressive asset allocation generates 29 percent more annual spending ability from one's retirement savings (excluding Social Security) and reduces downside risk by 33 percent."[38]
- The American College of Financial Servicesin 2019: "A stable income is often the difference between living well and living in a state of perpetual worry. And this truth doesn't change just because someone retires."[39]
- *Time Magazine* in 2012 "A new study in a land of grumps reveals that retirees with a guaranteed lifetime income stream can find true happiness" and "Securing at least a base level of lifetime income should be every retiree's priority—at least if they want to live happily ever after."[40]

37   Gal Wettstein, Alicia H. Munnell, Wenliang Hou, and Nilufer Gok, "The Value of Annuities" Working Paper 2021-5, March 2, 2021 (Chestnut Hill, MA: Center for Retirement Research at Boston College), https://crr.bc.edu/the-value-of-annuities/.

38   "How to Optimize Retirement Income," January 21, 2025, BlackRock, https://www.blackrock.com/us/individual/insights/retirement/optimize-retirement-income

39   "How Annuities Can Increase Happiness in Retirement," WealthManagement.com, Sponsored by the American College of Financial Services, December 16, 2019, https://www.wealthmanagement.com/retirement/how-annuities-can-increase-happiness-in-retirement

40   Dan Kadlec, "Lifetime Income Stream Key to Retirement Happiness," *Time Magazine,* July 30, 2012. https://business.time.com/2012/07/30/lifetime-income-stream-key-to-retirement-happiness/,

- *The Wall Street Journal* in 2005: "The Secret to a Happier Retirement: Friends, Neighbors and a Fixed Annuity."[41]

Remember to factor in Social Security funding in your bucket system. Remember, the SSA can't advise you on strategies and how to optimize Social Security. When you're taking Social Security, it may account for 40–45 percent of your retirement fund. It's not that much. With the way things are going, if benefits get cut or inflation keeps rising, that percentage will go down.

Remember that what order you take that money out and which vehicles you take it out of make a difference. These decisions directly affect your retirement tax burden and how long your money is going to last.

Let's close out this section by having you think about your retirement number. Case study Robert's shocking $2.27 million health care number drives home the fact that planning is essential. Your retirement number should be shocking, too, but in a good way. That's how much money you'll need for a financially secure retirement. That big number is broken down into needs, wants, and wishes for every phase of retirement. For most clients, we start with the needs to give them confidence that they're going to be financially stable for the rest of their lives.

---

41 Jonathan Clements, "The Secret to a Happier Retirement: Friends, Neighbors and a Fixed Annuity," *The Wall Street Journal*, July 27, 2005, https://www.wsj.com/articles/SB112241804795796704.

Generosity is the cornerstone of fulfillment and prosperity.

———

CHAPTER 6

Generous Giving: The Key to Retirement Happiness

Moms across the world have always taught us that it's better to give than to receive. I want to emphasize the importance of giving from the heart, not because you feel obligated but because it feels so incredibly good. Ralph Waldo Emerson famously said, "You cannot do a kindness too soon because you never know how soon it will be too late."

Generosity is the cornerstone of fulfillment and prosperity. For centuries, this timeless value has been revered across cultures and religions. In the context of financial planning and wealth management, generosity plays a crucial role in shaping one's legacy and personal fulfillment.

The Personal Benefits of Generosity

Generosity, the act of giving freely without expecting anything in return, is a simple concept, but the impact is profound and far reaching. It affects not only the recipient but also the giver and society as a whole.

Engaging in acts of kindness and giving can lead to a number of benefits.

Improved mental and emotional well-being. Studies have shown that being generous can boost happiness and reduce stress. When we give to others, our brain releases endorphins, dopamine, oxytocin, and serotonin, chemicals that promote a feeling of satisfaction and well-being.[42] Giving also boosts feelings of gratitude (how wonderful that you have extra to give) and helps you shift from a scarcity mindset to an abundance mindset.

Enhanced relationships. Generosity fosters a sense of trust and strengthens bonds between individuals. It encourages a sense of community and can lead to a more supportive and interconnected social network.

Personal growth and self-esteem. Giving to others can enhance one's sense of purpose and identity. It can lead to personal growth as individuals reflect on their values and the impact they wish to have on the world.

42 "Kindness Is Good for Mental Health and Overall Well-Being," Barnstable Community, Cape Cod Regional Government, November 13, 2023, https://www.capecod.gov/2023/11/13/kindness-is-good-for-mental-health-and-overall-well-being.

What the Bible Says about Generosity

A large amount of financial wisdom can be found in the old teachings. Many Biblical verses encourage generosity and kindness as generosity will be returned to us by God.

Money doesn't have a life. It cannot act on its own. It cannot do good deeds, and it cannot commit crimes. Basically, it's neither good nor bad. It is neutral.

Money can only do what you tell it to do. It's nothing but a tool. You decide whether to put it to good use or not.

Money is not the root of all evil, as some people believe; rather, it's the love of money that is the root of all evil (**1 Timothy 6:10, paraphrased**).

When it comes to money, we will either worship wealth or worship with our wealth.

Read that again. There's a big difference between the two.

It is righteous to practice generosity with our family, friends, and community as scripture inspires. We gain favor with God by being voluntarily charitable, and we produce goodwill among our fellow humans and foster a society of benevolence and compassion.

May this collection of a few of the scriptures on generosity shed some light on the importance and benefit of being generous with the blessings God has given us.

One gives freely, yet grows all the richer; another withholds what he should give, and only suffers want (**Proverbs 11:24, ESV**).

This is how we know what love is: Jesus Christ laid down his life for us. And we ought to lay down our lives for our brothers and sisters. If anyone has material possessions and sees a brother or sister in need but has no pity on them, how can the love of God be in that person? Dear children, let us not love with words or speech but with actions and in truth (**1 John 3:16–18, NIV**).

Remember this: Whoever sows sparingly will also reap sparingly, and whoever sows generously will also reap generously. Each of you should give what you have decided in your heart to give, not reluctantly or under compulsion, for God loves a cheerful giver. And God is able to bless you abundantly, so that in all things at all times, having all that you need, you will abound in every good work (**2 Corinthians 9:6–8, NIV**).

In everything I did, I showed you that by this kind of hard work we must help the weak, remembering the words the Lord Jesus himself said: "It is more blessed to give than to receive" (**Acts 20:35, NIV**).

Command those who are rich in this present world not to be arrogant nor to put their hope in wealth, which is so uncertain, but to put their hope in God, who richly provides us with everything for our enjoyment. Command them to do good, to be rich in good deeds, and to be generous and willing to share.

In this way they will lay up treasure for themselves as a firm foundation for the coming age, so that they may take hold of the life that is truly life (**1 Timothy 6:17–19, NIV**).

Good will come to those who are generous and lend freely, who conduct their affairs with justice (**Psalm 112:5, NIV**).

Whoever shuts their ears to the cry of the poor will also cry out and not be answered (**Proverbs 21:13, NIV**).

A generous person will prosper; whoever refreshes others will be refreshed (**Proverbs 11:25, NIV**).

Generosity in Financial Planning

Incorporating generosity into financial planning is about more than charitable giving; it's about creating a financial strategy that reflects one's values and desire to make a positive difference. Generosity in financial planning can include the following:

Estate Planning

Designing an estate plan with generosity in mind can ensure your wealth supports the causes and people you care about most, even after you're gone.

Strategic Philanthropy

By working with financial advisors, you can create a philanthropic strategy that helps to maximize the impact of your donations through tax-efficient giving and aligning with effective organizations.

Family Legacy

Teaching the next generation about the importance of generosity can help instill values that will last a lifetime and shape the family's legacy.

Generosity and Community Impact

Generosity has the power to transform communities in so many ways:

Support Vital Causes

Donations can fund research, support education, provide disaster relief, and more, leading to significant advancements and support for those in need.

Inspire Others

Acts of generosity often have a ripple effect, inspiring others to give and contribute to a culture of kindness and support.

Drive Social Change

Generous contributions to social causes can lead to systemic changes, addressing root problems and improving society for future generations.

What Ron Blue Has to Say about Generosity

Ron Blue is a top authority on personal finance from a Biblical perspective. He is one of my mentors and sources of inspiration. Ron wrote:

> One of my favorite stories about perspective comes from the Old Testament. After the Israelites had crossed the Red Sea, God led them to the Promised Land. Moses sent twelve spies into the land, and ten of them came back with weak knees and fearful hearts. Only two of them, Joshua and Caleb, saw the people already in the Promised Land from God's perspective and believed that He would allow the Israelites to have victory over them.
>
> As the rest of the spies quaked in fear, the two men with a different perspective said, "The land we passed through and explored is exceedingly good. If the LORD is pleased with us, He will lead us into that land, a land flowing with milk and honey, and will give it to us. Only do not rebel against the LORD. And do not be afraid of the people of the land, because we will swallow them up. Their protection is gone, but the LORD is with us. Do not be afraid of them" (Numbers 14:7b – 9; NIV). Because Joshua and Caleb saw the land as the Lord's and the battle as the Lord's and the victory as the Lord's, they had great confidence in facing a formidable foe.
>
> Money can be a formidable foe in our lives. Concerns about debt, provision for our families, economic uncertainty, future goals, and unexpected expenses can feel to us like giants in a land we dare not enter (Num-

149

bers 13:33). However, I believe that generosity is the key to changing our perspective of money. When we give to those in need, we acknowledge God's ownership and His power and His provision. We are able to remember that God will provide for us as He uses us as agents of provision in other people's lives. Our perspectives change when we give generously. We no longer fear the uncertainty of what lies ahead financially; rather, we can embrace the future with a surrendered heart.

Through generosity we can break the power that money has over us and is a path to true financial freedom. That generosity is something we consider to be a key to financial contentment and freedom.

So, as you consider the place of giving in your own life, ask yourself the heart question. The fact is: giving generously will never make the most financial sense. The fact is: even your most generous gifts will not alleviate a large part of the world's suffering. However, the fact is: giving generously toward God's purposes will draw your heart to Him in ways that nothing else can. Nothing.

As you chart a path toward financial wisdom by saving, controlling debt, having a budget, and setting goals, don't miss the chance to chart a simultaneous path toward the heart of God by giving generously.

May God's peace encourage you as you pursue financial freedom and depend on His Truth.[43]

---

43   Ron Blue, "A Generosity Perspective," Ron Blue Institute, April 4, 2022, https://ronblueinstitute.com/article/a-generosity-perspective/.

As we navigate our financial journeys, let us remember the power of generosity and the role it plays in creating a happier, more connected, and prosperous world.

A Giving Story: The Holiday Pantry

Peter and Emily wanted to teach their kids, fourteen-year-old Brianna and ten-year-old Kristina, about the importance of generous from-the-heart giving. The parents went grocery shopping, and this time, in addition to the family's regular staples, they bought as many non-perishable goods as they could that were earmarked for donation. These included canned vegetables, spaghetti sauce, sun-dried tomatoes, canned tuna and chicken, vegetable soup boxes, chicken broth, granola bars, cornbread mix, beans and lentils, canned stew, and brown rice. They also bought extra spices, dried fruit, and a large assortment of special non-perishable items they knew the kids would love: a bag of marshmallows, boxes of cookies, hot cocoa mix, applesauce, juice boxes, chocolate bars, assorted candies, and their favorite snack packs of mandarin orange slices.

Shortly before Christmas, Peter and Emily announced to the kids that the family would be donating food to the local food pantry. Each child was given a large basket and asked to pick some foods from the pantry that a needy family would appreciate as part of their special holiday meal.

The kids immediately got to work. They looked at the things they liked to eat and the things they didn't like. Both sisters started filling their baskets with food items they didn't like: canned veggies, beans, rice, granola bars, dried tomatoes, chicken broth. Their favorite treats were conspicuously absent from their donation baskets.

Once the baskets were full, Peter drove the girls to deliver their baskets to the food pantry while Emily went to the store to replenish the items the kids had donated. After delivering their baskets, the girls didn't have much to say on the matter. They were more excited about their own Christmas celebrations.

That night Peter and Emily surprised the kids with dinner made up entirely of foods that the girls had donated. The girls complained loudly. "Creamed corn and lentils?" whined little Kristina. "That's gross!" Brianna pouted and said, "Mom, seriously, what is this? It doesn't taste like anything. And why are we having granola bars for dessert?"

"This dinner is exactly what you donated to those needy families who can't afford a special Christmas dinner," Peter said. "We wanted to show you what it's like when people give generously but only because they think they have to. Do you expect anyone to be happy with this? You guys kept all the treats for yourself and donated the things you don't like. Imagine you're sitting at their table and it's Christmas. Sure, you're grateful that you have food, but is it food you like? Is it food your kids would like? Is it special? Wouldn't you be so much happier if some kind person wanted to share something special with you?"

Brianna and Kristina burst into tears. They hadn't thought of it that way. The girls immediately jumped out of their seats and filled a large box with treats that they knew would light up a family's festive dinner: spices, cookies, cocoa mix, marshmallows, dried fruit, chocolate, juice boxes, candies, and their beloved mandarin orange slices. Peter and Emily could hear the girls chattering excitedly as they sifted through the pantry. The girls brought the overflowing box back to the dinner table, where they proudly announced that this was the Christmas treat box they wanted to donate, and they were really sorry for being so stingy before.

The next morning the girls piled into the car and were knocking at the food pantry doors five minutes before it opened. On the way home the girls both remarked at how good it felt to make someone's Christmas special.

The lesson here is that giving should be on par with what you want to receive. I'm not saying that most people are stingy, but if they're giving out of a sense of obligation, they often give less (in terms of quantity and quality) than what they themselves would like to receive.

Never give out of guilt or obligation. Give lovingly. You don't have to give money if that's going to cause you stress or cause you to give grudgingly. You can give time and talents, and that costs nothing. Lightening someone's burden by doing one small thing can be a huge help for them.

If you get in the habit of donating a small amount when you don't have money, I'm confident that one day, when your wealth grows, you'll be able to donate more, and you'll do so without any anxiety because you're used to it. It's just what you do.

Giving ties into what you want to get out of retirement. What makes you happy? Revisit your passions. What can you do in that area to help others?

Give money or give things if you can, but your time and talents are priceless treasures too. Giving doesn't have to cost you anything other than your time.

We always hear about the importance of serving, but unfortunately, this word has a negative association. We think of it as being subservient to someone, less than, and serving also implies hard work. Jesus came here to serve. He wasn't beneath serving, and he lovingly washed people's feet. The head monk in a Buddhist monastery is the one who cleans the toilets.

Our society has become more selfish. It's more about us versus others. When people hear things that aren't about them, they turn off that naturally generous part of their being.

Giving doesn't mean that you lose while the recipient gains. Giving can be an important part of the happiness side of retirement. And when we talk about the happiness factor, yes, we're talking about your happiness, but it can include increasing the happiness of others too. If you make your community a happier place, then you're going to be happier living in that community. You don't have to give money to the orphanages in Africa if that's not your passion. What about your own neighborhood? What about your own community, where you can do something that will make you proud to be part of it?

We hear people say that money can't buy happiness. In fact, people of meager means who then came into money say that they were happier back when they had nothing. Maybe they were struggling and living through rough times—I definitely don't want to minimize their situation—but their lives were simpler and more focused on what matters, not on keeping up with the Joneses.

A Giving Story: The Businessman and the Fisherman

A young, wealthy businessman went on vacation to a Greek island. Day after day he relaxed on the beach, decompressing from his stressful job. He spent his days watching a fisherman in a beat-up dinghy pulling in his nets and then carrying bags of fish up the long hill to the village.

After about a week, the businessman walked up to the fisherman. "I see you're only catching half a dozen fish every day," he said. "If you get a bigger boat and bigger nets, you could catch more fish. If you catch more fish, you could make more money. Then you could spend more time relaxing on the beach like me."

"Sir, I'm a simple man," the fisherman replied. "I don't have a head for business like you do. But I do know this. If I get a new boat and new nets, I'll have to go into debt. It would take many years for me to catch and sell enough fish to repay that debt. Yes, I will catch more fish, but I will also have to work so much harder, and I'm getting to be an old man. My boat still works. My nets still work. I only fish for a few hours every day. I'm happy catching enough fish for my family, some for the village priest, some for my deaf brother, and some for the old widow up the road. I don't wish to make money from my fish. I wish to spend time with my family and my brothers and maintain the garden at the church. I'm a simple man with few needs, but I'm a happy man."

The businessman pondered this long and hard. His own salary was beyond generous, and he had all the perks anyone could ask for. But he was only allowed three weeks of vacation in a calendar year. He was heavily in debt from his mortgage on a fancy house, his ski condo, and his expensive cars and watches. He rarely thought about giving, and only donated out of obligation when the company encouraged employees to do so at Christmas.

Who's happier? the businessman thought. In his heart, he knew.

Society wants us to achieve more, amass more, but here we have this simple fisherman who catches enough fish for his family and a few villagers. He has no need to enrich his life with material things. He's happy to give what little he has: fish and the time it takes to beautify the church yard.

You don't often hear financial planners talking about the happiness that comes from giving, but it has been an important part of my life, and I believe generosity is central to a happy retirement. You have to have enough money to cover your expenses and have a bit left over, but as we can see from the fisherman's example, the happiness factor comes from a simple life that centers on giving.

Everything that you have done thus far financially can allow you to fully experience the happiness that comes from devoting your life to giving. Retirees are in a special and coveted position. They may have time to volunteer at the animal shelter. They may have the means to give free piano lessons to low-income kids. They may have the expertise to start a community garden at a local park or to conduct a used battery drive. They may have the wisdom to teach skills to single moms in domestic abuse shelters or to mentor underserved high school kids and teach them interview skills and how to dress for success.

I've heard so many clients say, "I would love to retire and do charity work." People say it, but few ever do it. Let's make a plan so you can do that thing that's tugging at your heart. Let's make it so you can answer the question, "What would you do if money were no object? What would you do with your days?"

Never give out of
guilt or obligation.
Give lovingly.

———

CONCLUSION

In this book, we've covered the basics of retirement planning: the why and the how. We've discussed timeless financial wisdom handed down to us through the ages as well as modern ways to grow and preserve your nest egg.

Section 1 discussed your goals in retirement: your retirement why. We began building a foundation of financial knowledge that will help you understand the retirement strategies outlined in section 2.

Section 2 gave you the nuts and bolts of wise retirement planning that make up The Retire Happy Framework™:

- Retirement risks that can derail your plans and ways to mitigate these risks
- The phases of retirement and their related funding strategies and key risk mitigation strategies

- Drawdown strategies that help ensure a consistent, steady retirement income for the duration of your retirement
- The principle of generous giving as the keystone to a confident retirement

Now that you have this knowledge, let me ask you: What's preventing you from living the retirement of your dreams?

Whether you lack a nest egg, a purpose, or a financial strategy, or you started too late, or you have high debt and risky investments, or you have a combination of these factors, the financial planners at Retire Wise, LLC can help. We can help guide you in creating a financial plan that is right for you so that you can feel confident about your retirement.

Together, we will create a comprehensive retirement plan that focuses on helping you achieve personal fulfillment, contentment, and financial security so that you can retire confidently. You deserve happiness in retirement. Let's make it happen!

MY STORY

When I was a kid, I was searching for life's purpose and joy, though I didn't realize it until I was older. We all have a God-given purpose in this life. Some people find it early, while others struggle all their lives. As the years went by, finding my unique purpose became more of a focus. And as my spiritual walk with Jesus became stronger and I leaned on Him more, my purpose started to make more sense. It ultimately brought me to my career and what I love to do.

I was in the eighth grade and was signed up to play the Stock Market Game with my class. Players are assigned pretend money and have to study and buy stock in companies based on real companies and the current real stock market. We played over the course of the year and eventually saw who gained the most. Some ended up with way less money than what they started with, some ended up with more, and some ended up with significantly more. Well, I won the Stock Market Game. I had the highest gains at a 48 percent yield. Needless to say, I was hooked.

People find it funny that from such a young age, I wanted to be a businessman and to own my own company. The urge started in kindergarten when I would take my parents' junk mail and other miscellaneous supplies and play office. It seemed to be in my blood and at my core.

In college I studied business, finance, and investments, as well as psychology, to help with the relational side of business. I was on the dean's list, eventually graduated, and felt like I was on my way.

I landed an interview with a prestigious investment firm in Atlanta and went through a grueling multi-week interview process. After a four-hour interview with the director—phew, that was tough—I got an offer the next day. I was on cloud nine and ready to conquer my career and the world.

Since graduating college, I had been living with my parents until I found a job. I told my parents the good news, and they said they had news for me as well. My dad's job was transferring him—my parents were moving to Florida. My heart sank. I was not moving to Florida! The problem was, in this type of job with an investment firm, you don't make any (or much) money for six to nine months as you train, get all your licenses, and learn the ropes. I needed to make money and have a place to live. I had to turn down my dream job.

Fortunately, I landed a job with a bank and quickly made my way into management. Within two years I was a department head and was promoted several times. But I still wasn't doing what I wanted, so I moved on to a technology company. The economy wasn't great, markets were in turmoil, and investment companies weren't hiring, unless you had a lot of previous experience. And they paid peanuts. There was still that whole "I need to eat" thing.

The technology job was with a financial technology (fintech) company working with banks, investment firms, etc. I applied my work ethic wherever I went and worked my way up in this company as well, eventually leading an entire product division and overseeing many product offerings. That company was bought out, and its culture drastically changed.

I still wasn't doing what I wanted. I wasn't fulfilled. I didn't see any opportunity to get into my dream career. I got recruited to another, even more advanced fintech company. I led a few departments there and built some great teams, but I wasn't happy with my career despite the success.

During this time, I had kept up with financial knowledge and certifications and had been helping people on the side with financial planning. I decided to get the rest of the licenses and certifications I needed in the investment and financial space and start a side gig. That's when I started my own LLC to feed that desire: Retire Wise, LLC.

It became harder and harder to concentrate on my day job since I loved my side gig, but I couldn't do both full time.

I was also teaching groups at my church about financial basics and providing education. It began to tug at me that I really loved to help people: to help them with their financial life and educate them along the way so they understand personal finance. I began to focus on full retirement planning, or comprehensive planning both financial and non-financial for retirement.

We all work hard our whole life, and everyone deserves a good retirement. I was seeing too many people who weren't ready, didn't have a plan, and were struggling to pay their basic bills. It became harder and harder to ignore the call to help and still do my day job.

I prayed about it and sought counsel from close friends and advisors. Everywhere I turned I was being called and shown to do this financial work in service of others. I took a leap of faith and quit my well-paying, successful corporate job. I would now focus full time on my company and my purpose—to help others plan for their happy retirement. The rest is history.

ABOUT THE AUTHOR

Founder | CEO | Licensed Financial Professional

My name is Shawn Maloney, and I am an independent financial planner and the owner and CEO of Retire Wise, LLC. With over twenty years of experience in the financial services industry, I have a passion for helping people ready themselves for retirement.

I started my career in financial technology and compliance before moving into insurance and financial planning roles. I then founded Retire Wise, LLC, in 2020. My insights have been featured in publications such as Yahoo Finance, USA Today, and Kiplinger, and on TV networks including NBC, ABC, FOX, and CBS.

As an independent financial advisor, I am committed to helping my clients pursue their goals. I aim to help clients reach a comfortable retirement lifestyle through comprehensive retirement plans. As an investment adviser representative, I have dedicated my career to helping ensure that individuals are equipped with the information and tools they need to help grow and preserve their retirement savings. My focus is on comprehensive and personalized retirement planning, including the important drawdown phase as well as accumulation to get ready, providing clients with a clear and understandable framework for the future. My team and I also consider the non-financial aspects of retirement as well, to assist with preparing a more complete plan.

Utilizing my transparent and comprehensive approach to planning, known as The Retire Happy Framework™, I help provide our clients with confidence about their future.

I hold a BBA in finance and investments from Georgia Southern University. In addition to helping people with retirement planning, I find solace in spending time with my family and giving back to my community and church. Join me on this journey towards creating a fulfilling retirement and let's make the most out of every day!

www.ingramcontent.com/pod-product-compliance
Lightning Source LLC
Chambersburg PA
CBHW030517210326
41597CB00013B/942